ESSENTIAL ELEMENTS for Strings

COMPREHENSIVE STRING METHOD

MICHAEL ALLEN • ROBERT GILLESPIE • PAMELA TELLEJOHN HAYES
ARRANGEMENTS BY JOHN HIGGINS

Congratulations for successfully completing Book 1 and welcome to Book 2 of *Essential Elements for Strings*! By now you are well aware of the benefits and joy of playing bass in the orchestra. The techniques you learned in Book 1 will help you reach a more advanced level in Book 2 that will make your musical experiences even more fun and exciting.

You can learn the new skills in the order they occur in Book 2, or you can master a particular skill at the time it most applies to your individual playing needs. Tabs appear on the sides of each page to help you quickly find the section or concept you need to practice.

There will be rewards for your effort! As you spend time learning more challenging material, the mastery of new skills will bring you even more joy in the years to come. Good luck, and best wishes for a lifetime of musical happiness!

Keys

Rhythms

To create an account, visit:
www.essentialelementsinteractive.com

Student Activation Code
E2DB-7457-1857-2683

ISBN 979-835013660-9

HAL•LEONARD®
A Muse Group Company

REVIEW

KEY SIGNATURE

Key of D

TIME SIGNATURE

4/4

NOTES

Whole | Half | Quarter

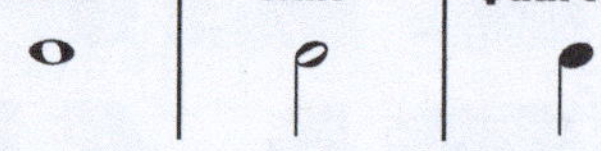

SLUR

Major Scale A Major Scale is a series of eight notes that follow a definite pattern of whole steps and half steps. Half steps appear only between scale steps 3-4 and 7-8. Every major scale has the same arrangement of whole steps and half steps.

1. TUNING TRACK

2. D MAJOR SCALE – Round *(When group A reaches ②, group B begins at ①)*

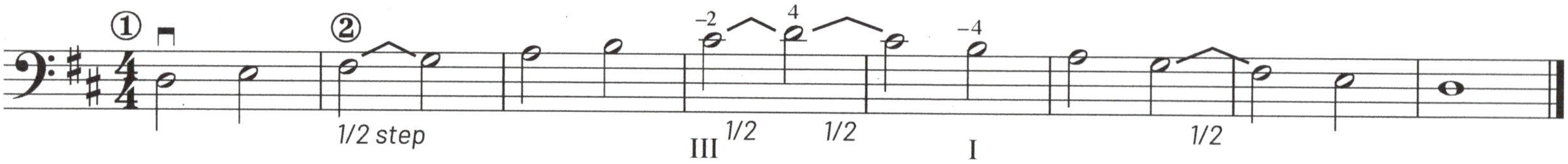

3. D MAJOR ARPEGGIO

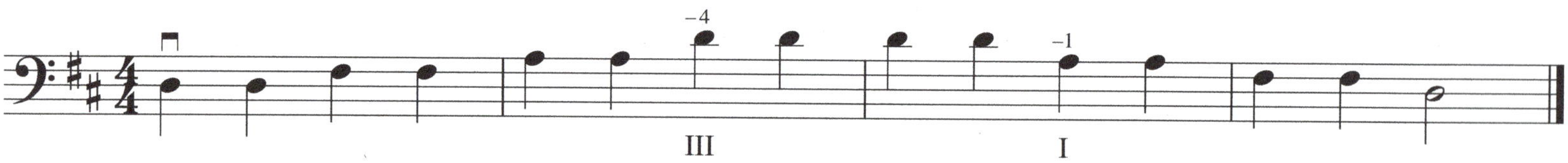

4. D MAJOR MANIA

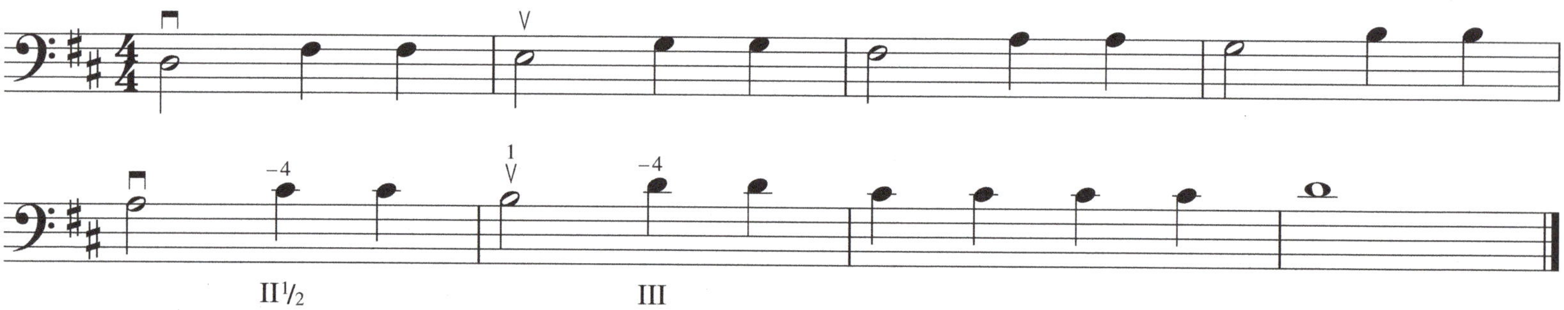

Legato Played in a smooth and connected style.

5. THEME FROM LONDON SYMPHONY

Franz J. Haydn (1732-1809)

REVIEW

Forte (*f*) **Piano (*p*)** **Bow Lift (,)**

TIME SIGNATURE 3/4

NOTES Dotted Half · Eighths

TIE

TEMPO MARKING Moderato

1st & 2nd ENDINGS 1. 2.

3/4 RHYTHMS

6. D MAJOR IN THREES

Dynamics

crescendo (cresc.) — Gradually increase volume.
decrescendo (decresc.) — Gradually decrease volume.

7. DYNAMIC CONTRASTS

HISTORY

Norwegian composer **Edvard Grieg** wrote *Peer Gynt Suite* for a play by Henrik Ibsen in 1875, the year before the telephone was invented by Alexander Graham Bell. "Morning" is a melody from *Peer Gynt Suite*. Music used in plays, or in films and television, is called **incidental music**.

8. MORNING (from Peer Gynt)

Edvard Grieg (1843–1907)

Moderato

9. BARCAROLLE

Jacques Offenbach (1819–1880)

Moderato

WORKOUTS

Tunneling
Slide your fingers up and down the fingerboard between 2 strings.

Ridin' The Rails
Slide up and down one string with your fingers.

Tappin' And Slidin'
Tap your fingers on any string, slide toward the other end of the fingerboard, and tap again.

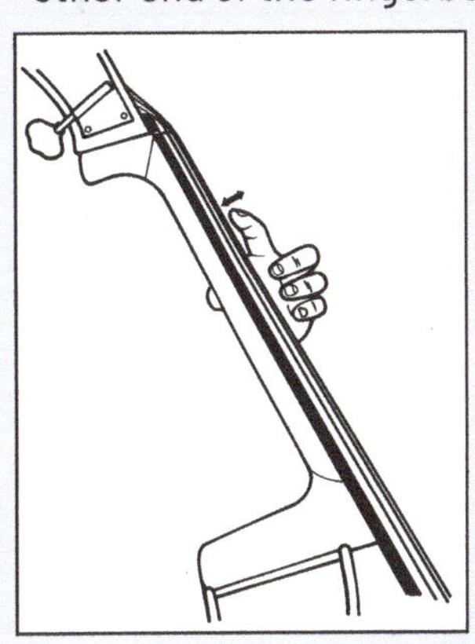

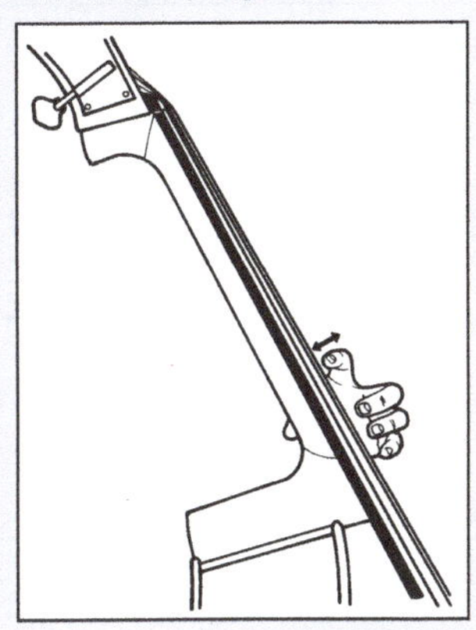

See inside front cover for information on accessing instructional videos.

REVIEW

KEY SIGNATURE

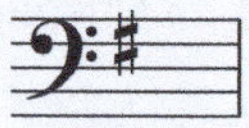

Key of G

HOOKED BOWING

TEMPO MARKING

Andante

10. G MAJOR SCALE – Round

11. G MAJOR ARPEGGIO

THEORY

Interval The distance between two notes is called an interval. Start with "1" on the lower note, and count each line and space between the notes. The number of the higher note is the distance, or name, of the interval.

12. SCALE INTERVALS

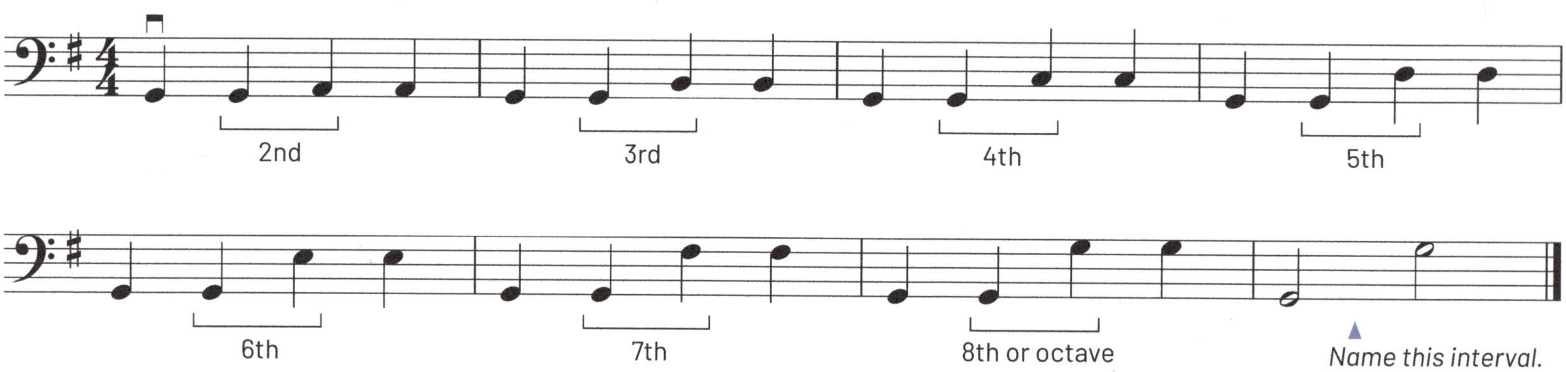

13. CHESTER

William Billings (1746–1800)

✔ Is your left hand shaped properly?

REVIEW

KEY SIGNATURE

Key of G *(Upper Octave - violin)*

TEMPO MARKING

Allegro

14. G MAJOR SCALE *(Upper Octave - violin)*

15. G MAJOR ARPEGGIO *(Upper Octave - violin)*

Intonation

Intonation is how well each note is played in tune.

16. INTONATION ENCOUNTER – Duet

17. THE OUTBACK

REVIEW

KEY SIGNATURE

Key of C

TIME SIGNATURE

STACCATO

18. C MAJOR SCALE

19. C MAJOR ARPEGGIO

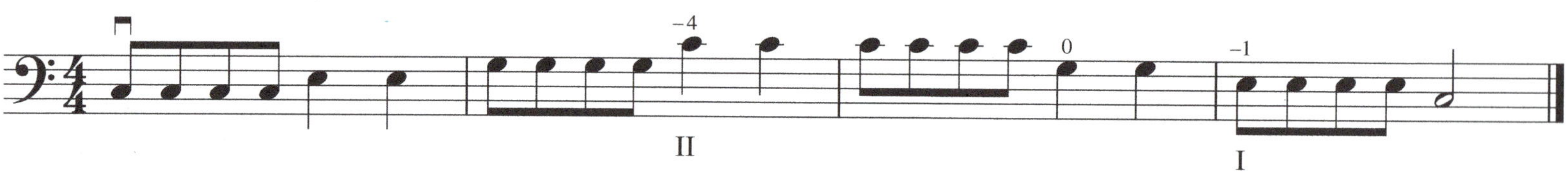

20. C MAJOR DUET

21. BINGO

Allegretto

✔ Check your bow hand. Are your fingers curved and is your thumb bent?

REVIEW

KEY SIGNATURE

Key of C *(Lower Octave – viola and cello)*

TIME SIGNATURE

C

TONE PRODUCTION

- place bow between bridge and fingerboard
- bow straight
- proper weight

22. C MAJOR SCALE – Round *(Lower Octave – viola and cello)*

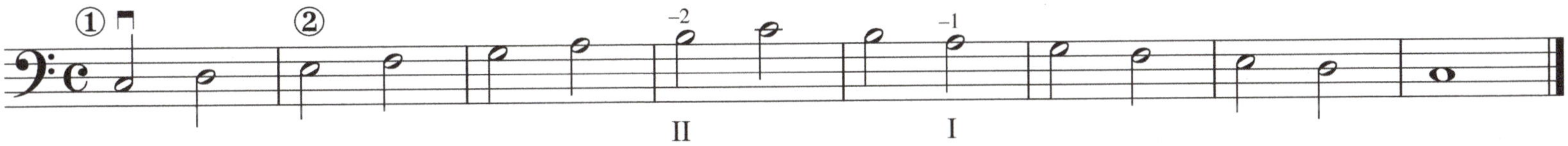

23. C MAJOR ARPEGGIO *(Lower Octave – viola and cello)*

24. C MAJOR MANIA

Dynamics

mp	*(mezzo piano)*	Play moderately soft.
mf	*(mezzo forte)*	Play moderately loud.

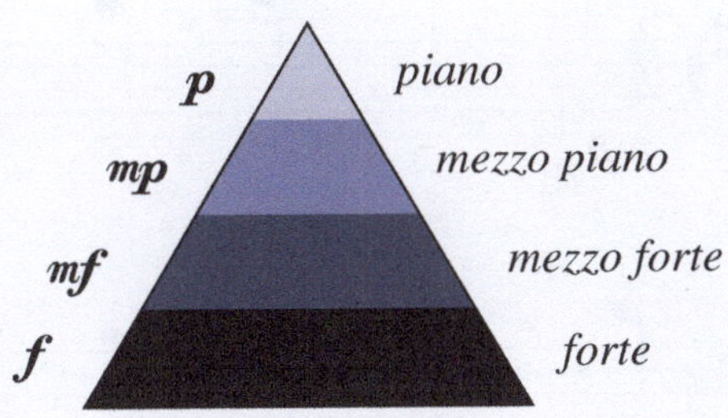

25. CROSSROADS

Moderato

CHANGING BOW SPEED

Change the bow speed according to the length of the note. When you have a longer note value, the bow speed should be slower. If there is a dotted half note on a down bow and a quarter note on an up bow, the speed of the bow must change.

Example:

Slow Bow → *Fast Bow*

26. THE DOT ALWAYS COUNTS

27. ALOUETTE

French Folk Song

Allegretto

28. RIGAUDON

Henry Purcell (1659–1695)

Moderato

29. ESSENTIAL CREATIVITY – CANDY MOUNTAIN ROCK

Make up your own dynamics and write them in the music. Play the line and describe how the dynamics change the sound.

Allegretto

Eighth Note & Eighth Rest

♪ = 1/2 beat of sound

𝄾 = 1/2 beat of silence

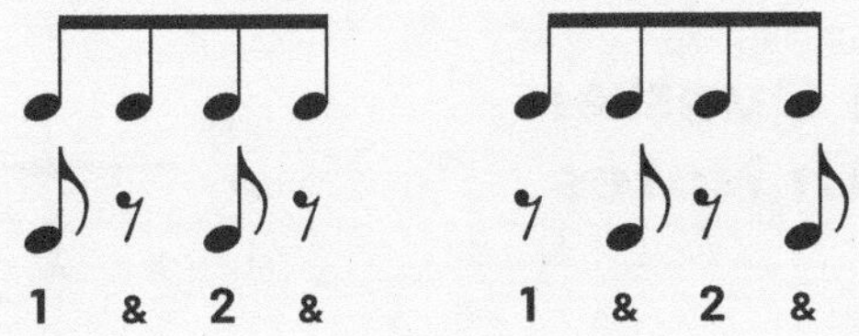

RHYTHMS

30. RHYTHM RAP ♪ 𝄾

Shadow bow and count before playing.

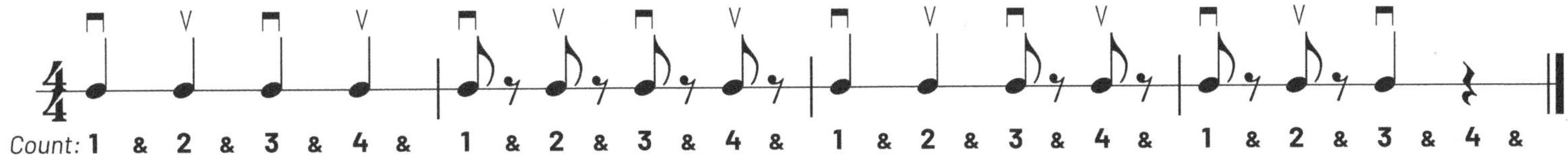

31. EIGHTH NOTES ON THE BEAT

32. SHORT AND SWEET

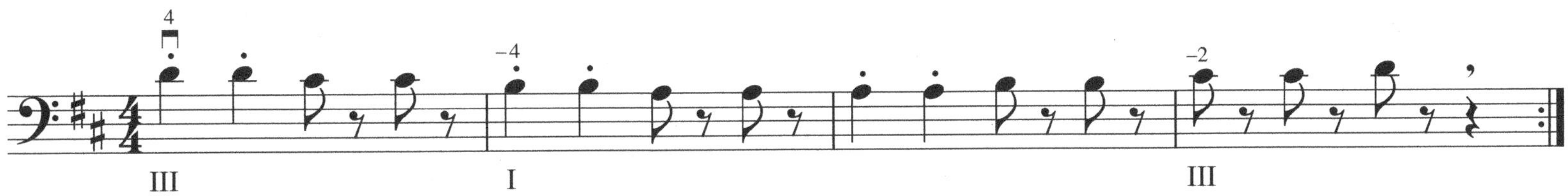

33. RHYTHM RAP 𝄾 ♪

Shadow bow and count before playing.

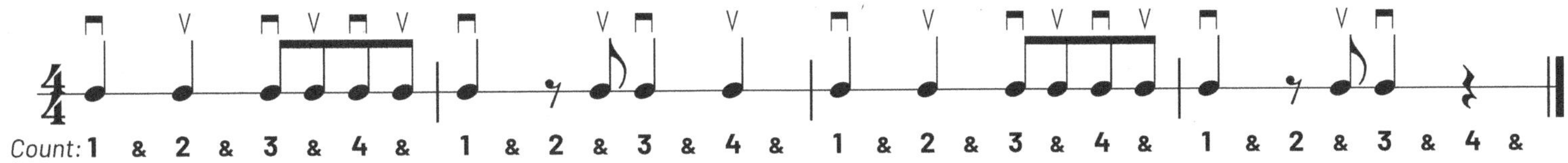

34. EIGHTH NOTES OFF THE BEAT

35. SUNNY DAY

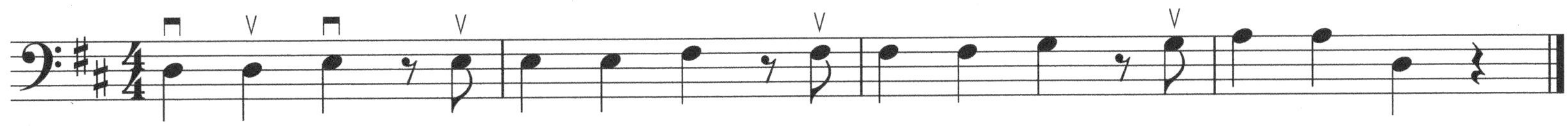

36. ESSENTIAL ELEMENTS QUIZ – JESSE JAMES

Folk Ballad from Missouri

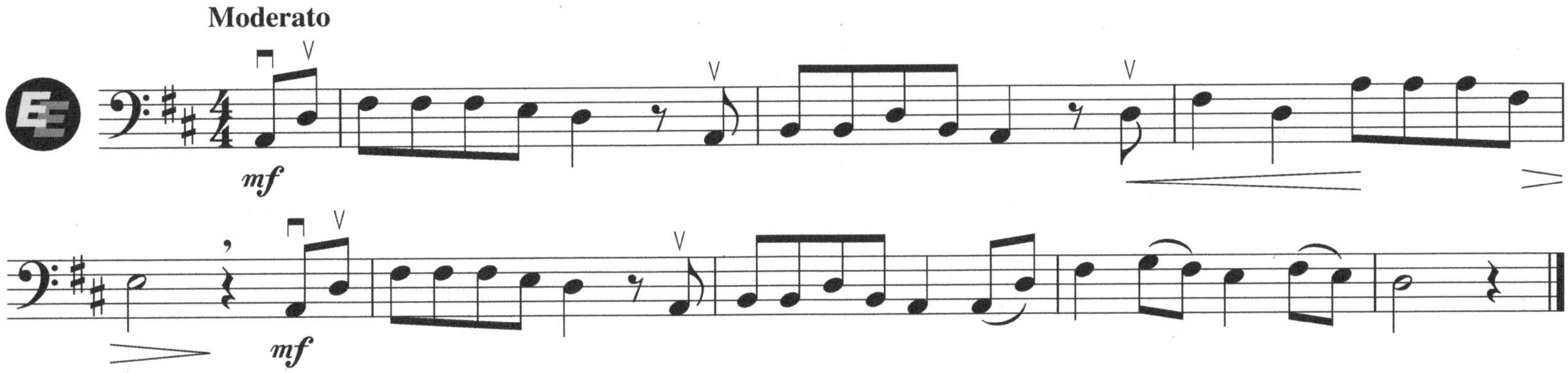

Dotted Quarter & Eighth Notes

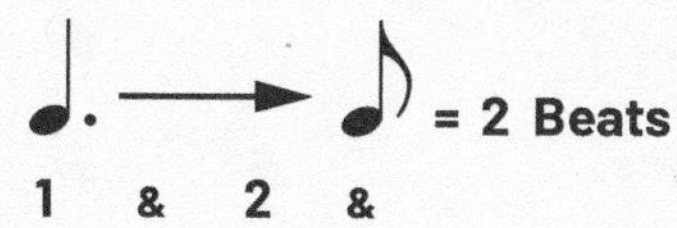

A **dot** adds half the value of the quarter note.

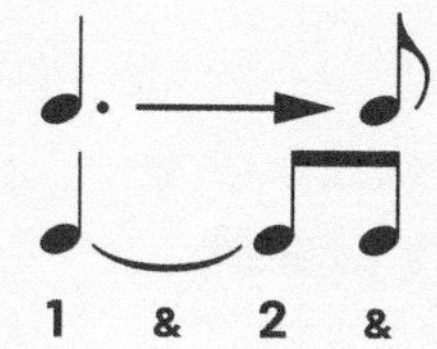

37. RHYTHM RAP

Shadow bow and count before playing.

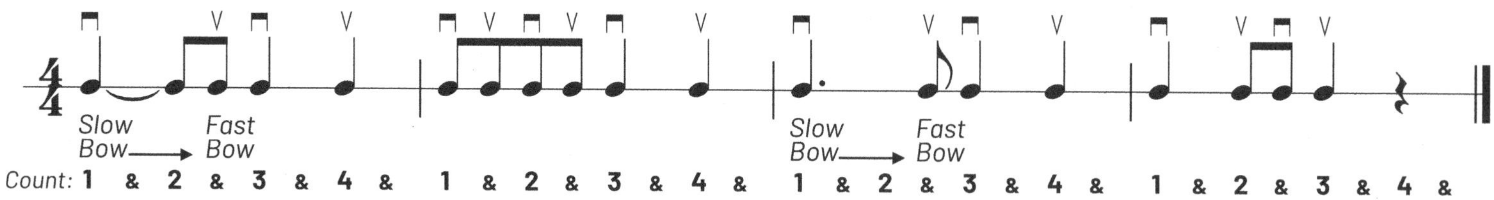

38. THE DOT COUNTS

39. WATCH THE DOT

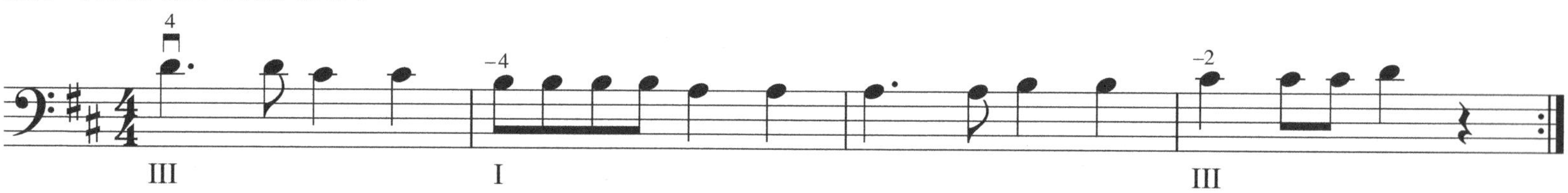

40. D MAJOR SEQUENCE

41. DOTS ON THE MOVE

Fermata

Hold the note (or rest) longer than normal.

42. D MAJOR BONANZA – Duet

43. A CAPITAL SHIP

American Folk Song

44. ESSENTIAL CREATIVITY

Create your own rhythms by penciling in a dot and a flag to change any two quarter notes from ♩ ♩ to ♩. ♪

45. HOOKED ON DOTS

Ritardando *ritard.* (or) *rit.* – Gradually slower.

46. THEME FROM NEW WORLD SYMPHONY

Antonin Dvorák (1841–1904)

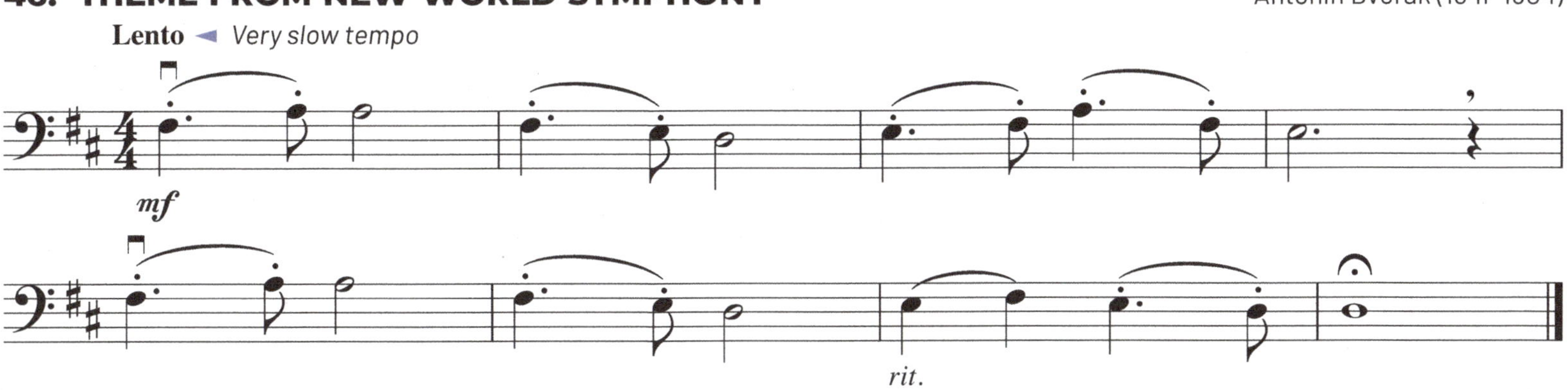

47. ESSENTIAL ELEMENTS QUIZ – RONDEAU

Jean-Joseph Mouret (1682–1738)

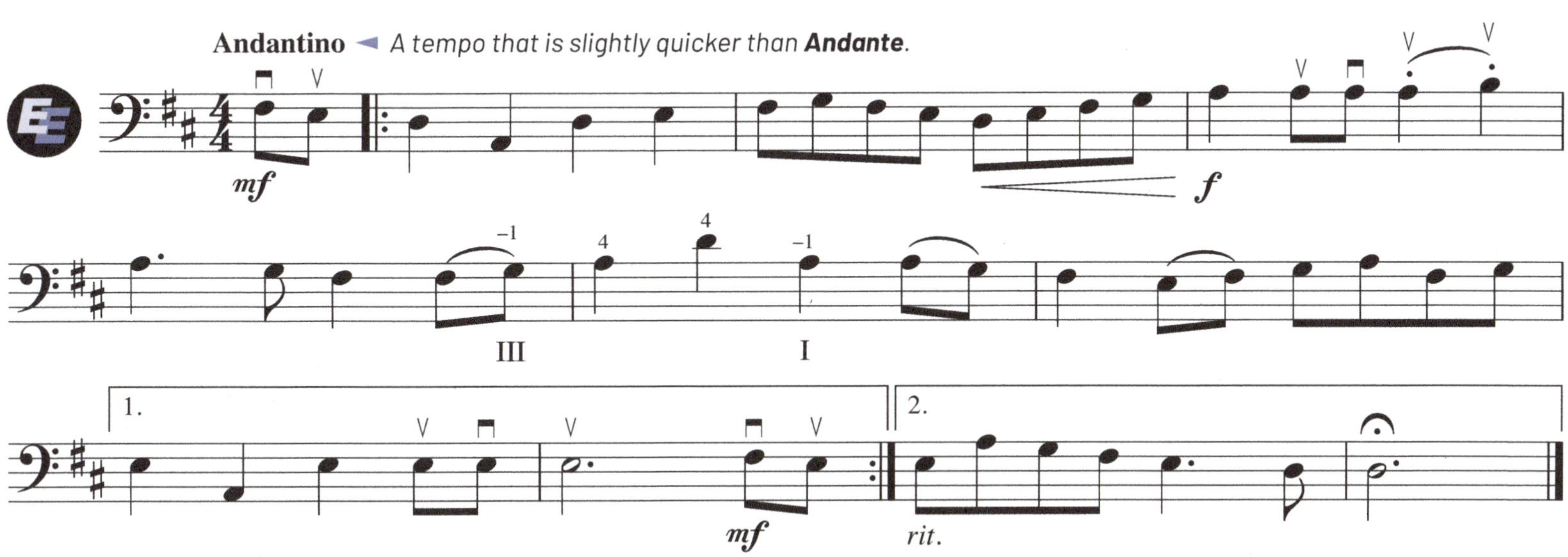

Team Work Great musicians give encouragement to their fellow performers. Violin, viola, and cello players will now learn a new challenging skill. The success of your orchestra depends on everyone's talent and patience. Play your best as members of these sections advance their musical technique.

Special Double Bass Exercise

Draw a note next to each printed note that will match the interval number shown. The note you draw can be higher or lower than the printed note. The first one is done for you.

2nd *(Example)* | 5th | 3rd | octave *(go lower only)* | 4th | 6th *(go lower only)* | 7th *(go lower only)*

Listening Skills Play what your teacher plays. Listen carefully.

48. LET'S READ "C♯" (C-sharp)

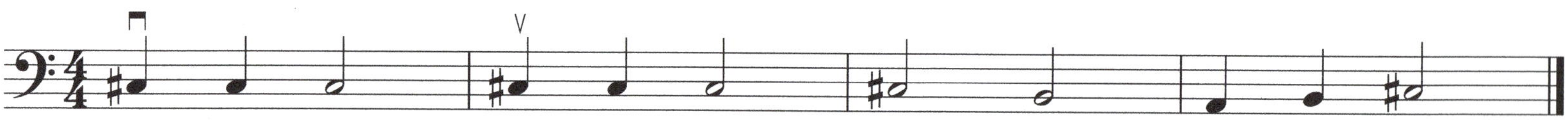

49. STAY SHARP

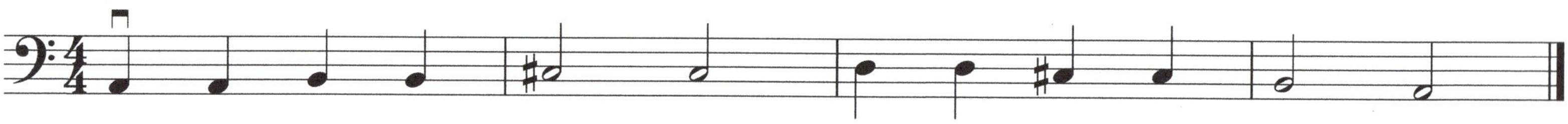

50. AT PIERROT'S DOOR

French Folk Song

Andante

51. HOT CROSS BUNS

Moderato

✔ Were your C♯'s in tune?

HALF POSITION ON THE G STRING

G♯

is played with 1 finger on the G string in half position (1/2).

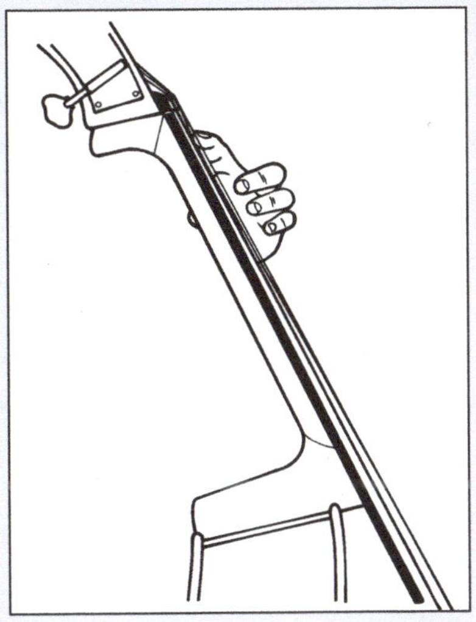

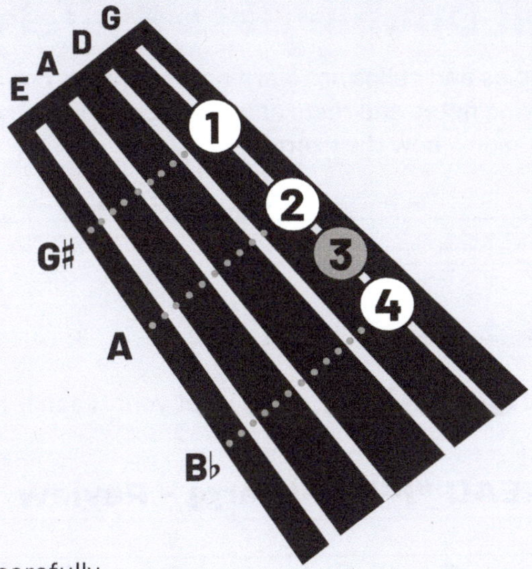

Listening Skills Play what your teacher plays. Listen carefully.

52. LET'S READ "G♯" (G-sharp)

53. REACHING OUT

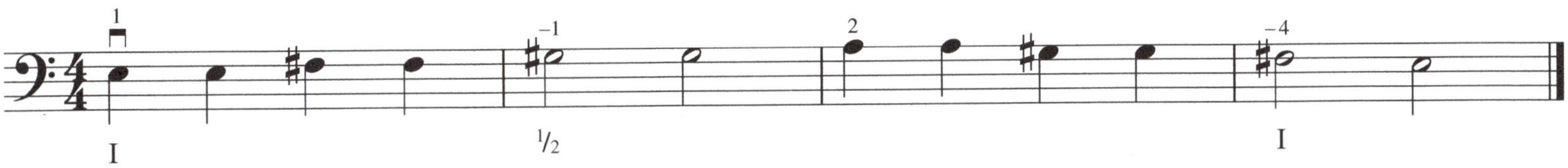

54. HIGHER AND HIGHER

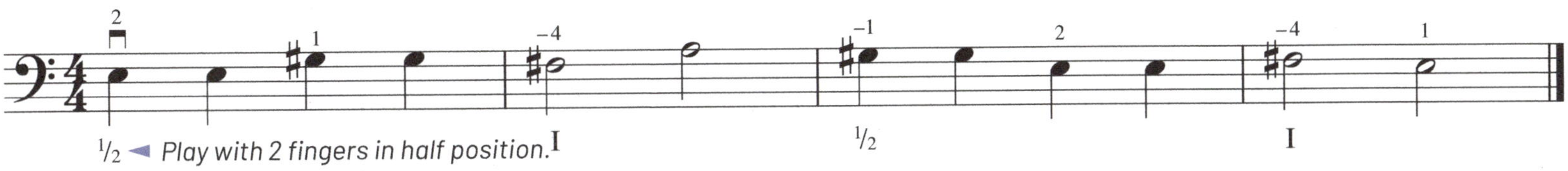

Key Signature A MAJOR

Play all F's as F♯ (F-sharp), all C's as C♯ (C-sharp), and all G's as G♯ (G-sharp).

55. A MAJOR SCALE

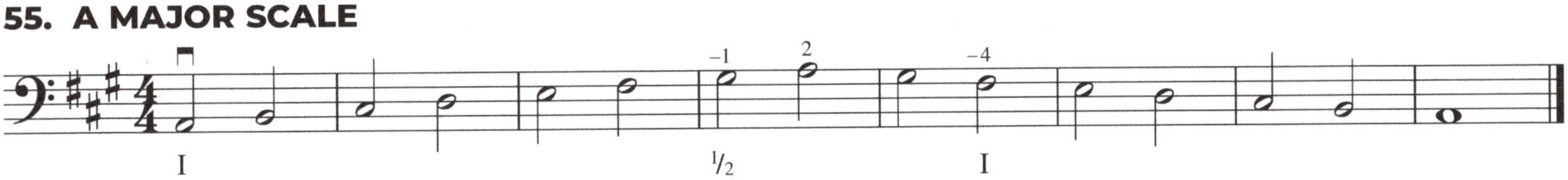

56. ESSENTIAL ELEMENTS QUIZ – A SONG FOR ANNE

LOWER OCTAVE OF D MAJOR (viola and cello)

Special Double Bass Exercise

While the violas and cellos are learning a new note, choose any one pitch on the staff and make up a rhythm exercise. Use each of the following notes and rests at least once (𝅗𝅥. 𝅗𝅥 ♩ ♪ 𝄼 𝄽 𝄾). Be sure to line up your notes and rests with the counting. After you finish, shadow bow the exercise.

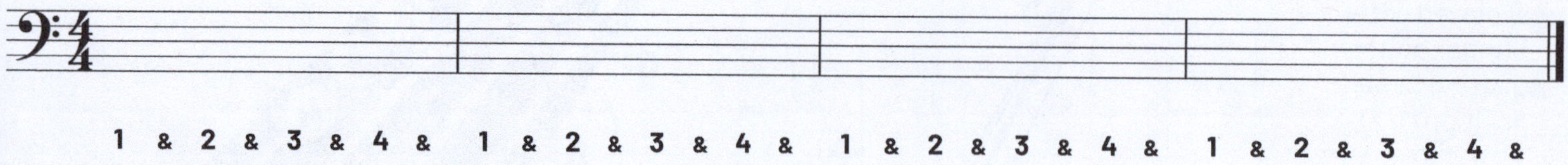

Listening Skills Play what your teacher plays. Listen carefully.

57. LET'S READ "F♯" (F-sharp) – Review

58. HIGH POINT

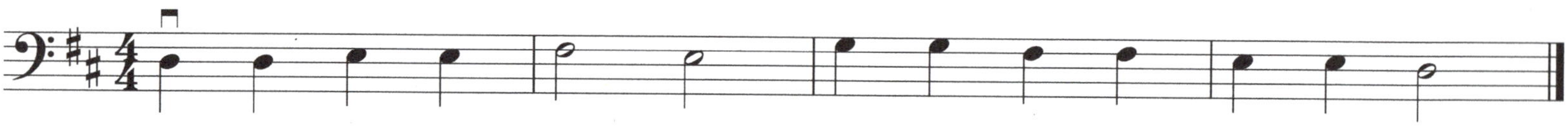

59. MAGNIFICENT MONTANA

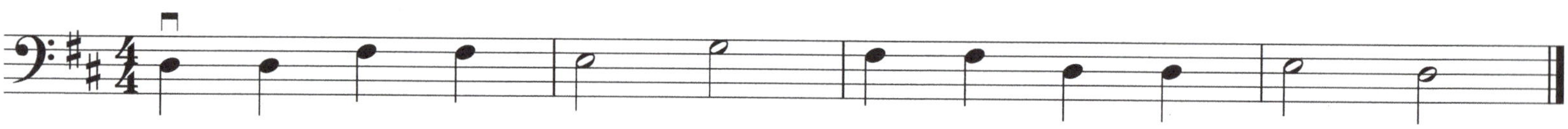

60. D MAJOR SCALE – Round

HISTORY

In the second half of the 1800s many composers tried to express the spirit of their own country by writing music with a distinct national flavor. Listen to and describe the music of Scandinavian and Spanish composers, and Russian composers such as Borodin, Tchaikovsky, and Rimsky-Korsakov. They often used folk songs and dance rhythms to convey their nationalism.

61. RUSSIAN FOLK TUNE

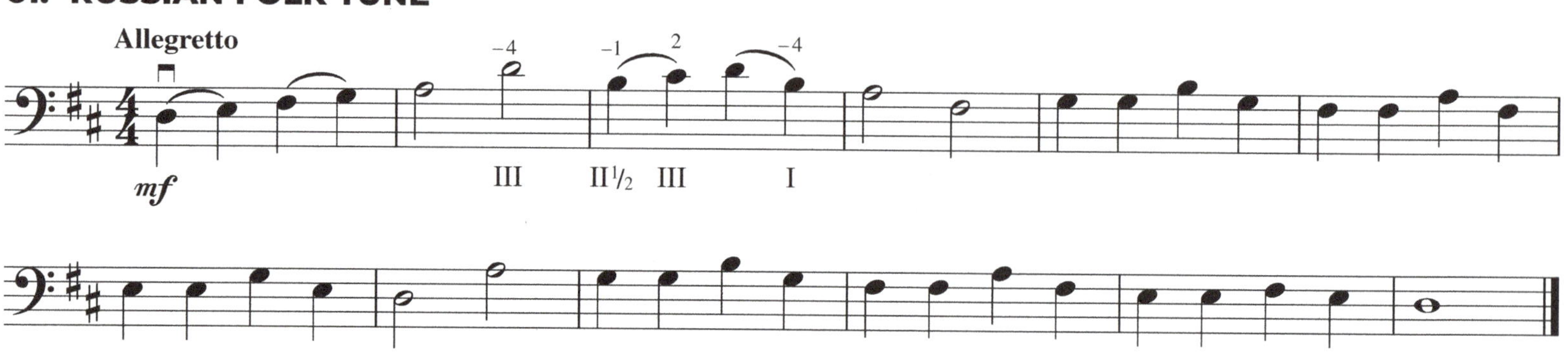

G♯ (G-SHARP) ON THE E STRING

G♯

is played with 4 fingers on the E string in first position (I).

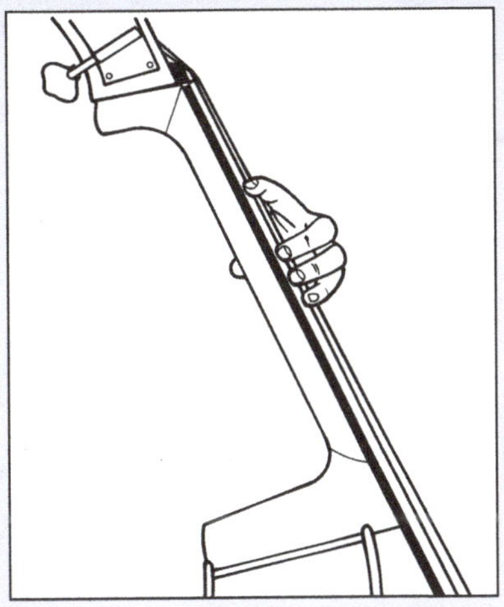

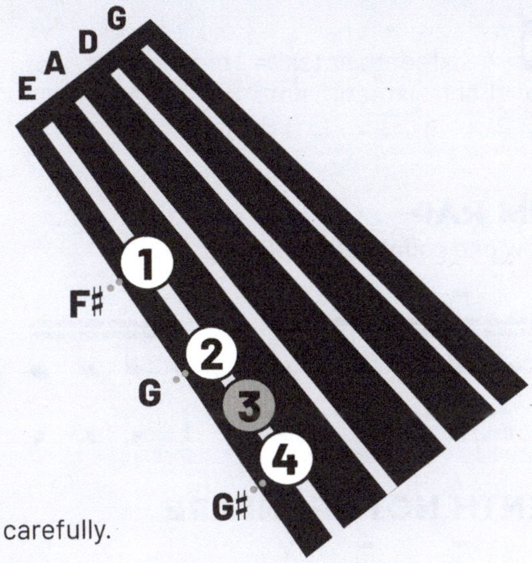

Listening Skills Play what your teacher plays. Listen carefully.

62. LET'S READ "G♯" (G-sharp)

63. A MAJOR SCALE

64. A MAJOR ARPEGGIO

65. THE FIG TREE

Accent 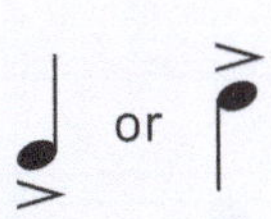 Emphasize the note. Add weight or increase the speed at the beginning of the bow stroke.

66. SITKA CITY

Russian Folk Song

Sixteenth Notes

4 sixteenth notes = 1 beat
Each sixteenth note = 1/4 beat

A single sixteenth note has 2 flags on the stem.

67. RHYTHM RAP

Shadow bow and count before playing.

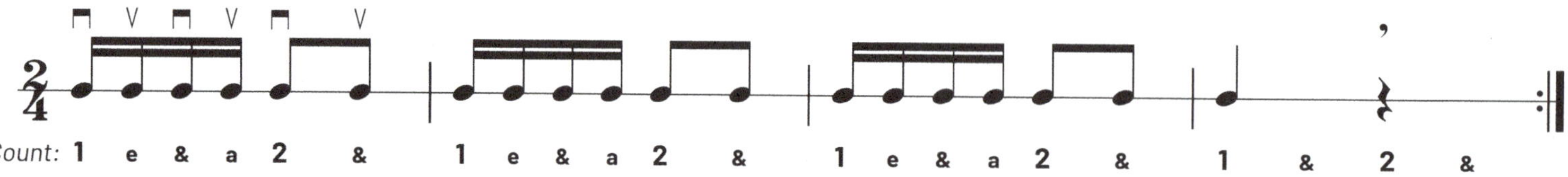

68. SIXTEENTH NOTE FANFARE

69. TECHNIQUE TRAX

70. SWEET SIXTEENTHS

Allegretto

71. MOCKINGBIRD

Alice Hawthorne (Septimus Winner) (1827–1902)

Moderato

Looking for some more fun music to play?
See the inside front cover for instructions on accessing recent popular Bonus Songs.

RHYTHMS

72. RHYTHM RAP

Shadow bow and count before playing.

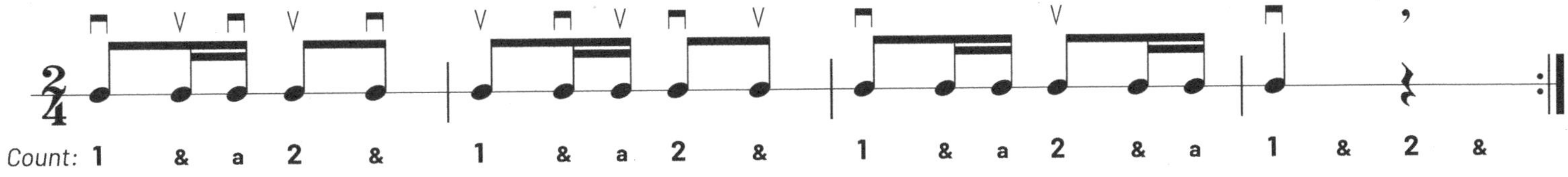

73. BLUEBERRY PIE

74. TECHNIQUE TRAX

75. RHYTHM RAP

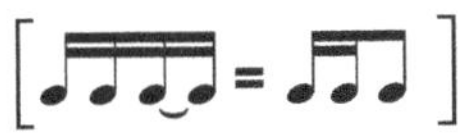

Shadow bow and count before playing.

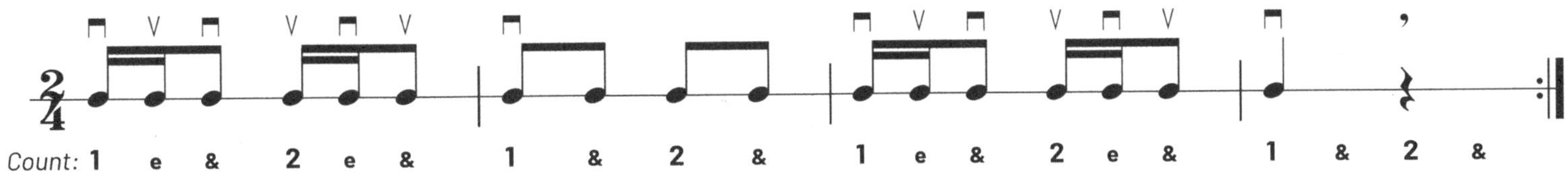

76. MARCHING ALONG

77. ON THE MOVE

78. RHYTHM ETUDE – Duet

79. ESSENTIAL ELEMENTS QUIZ – RHYTHM ROUND-UP

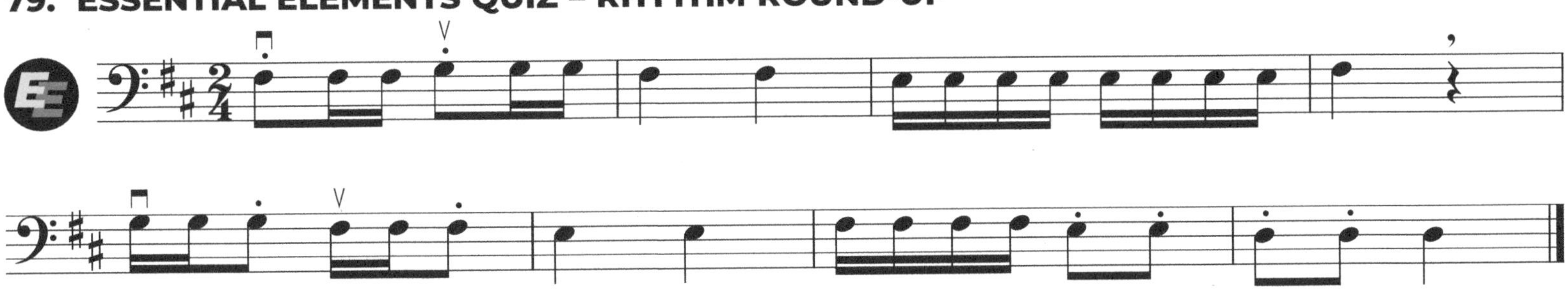

80. RHYTHM RAP

Shadow bow and count before playing.

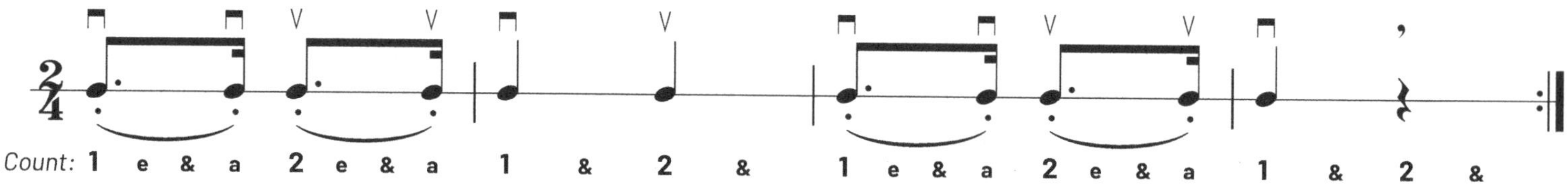

81. TECHNIQUE TRAX

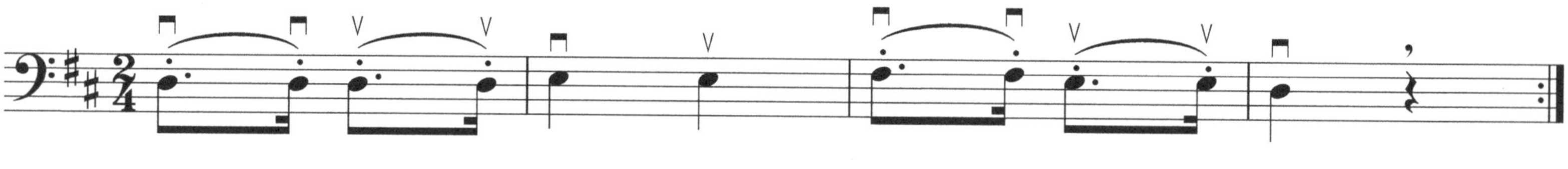

82. HOOKED ON D MAJOR

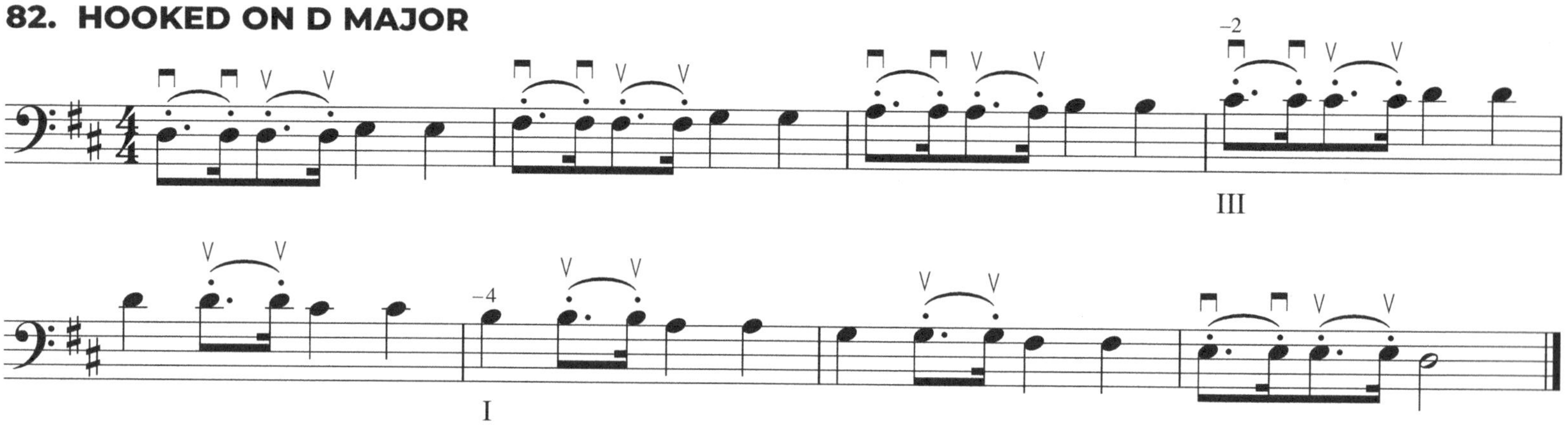

83. THE MOUNTAIN CLIMBER

84. KEEP IT SHORT

85. ESSENTIAL CREATIVITY

Write a D Major scale using any of the following rhythms:  *Perform your composition for the class.*

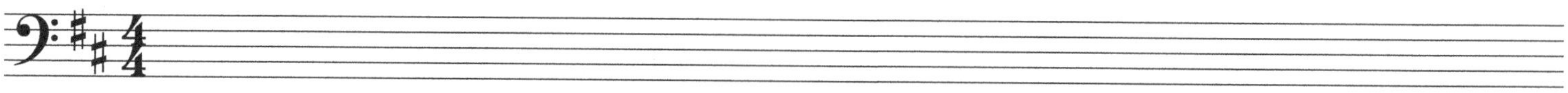

Syncopation

Syncopation occurs when an accent or emphasis is given to a note that is not on a strong beat. This type of "off-beat" feel is common in many popular and classical styles.

THEORY

RHYTHMS

86. RHYTHM RAP

Shadow bow and count before playing.

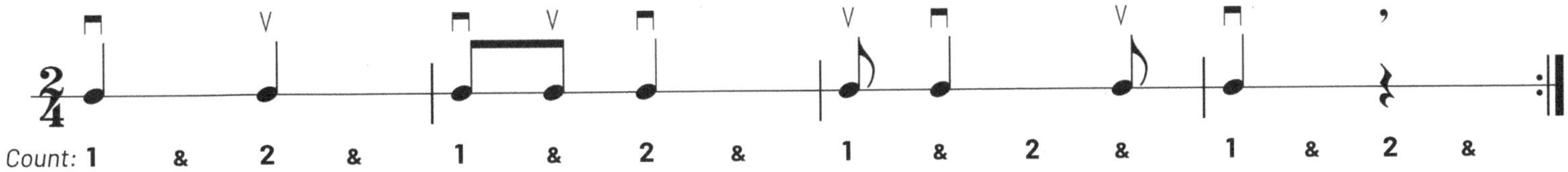

87. SYNCOPATION TIME

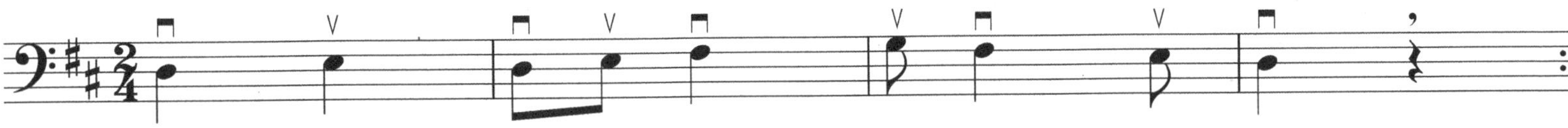

88. MIRROR IMAGE

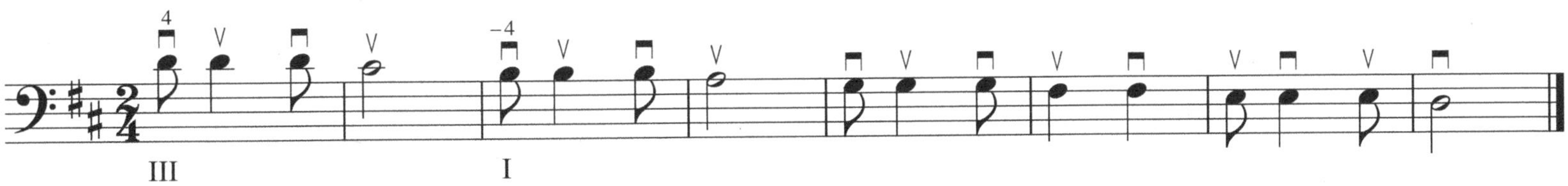

89. CHILDREN'S SHOES

African American Spiritual

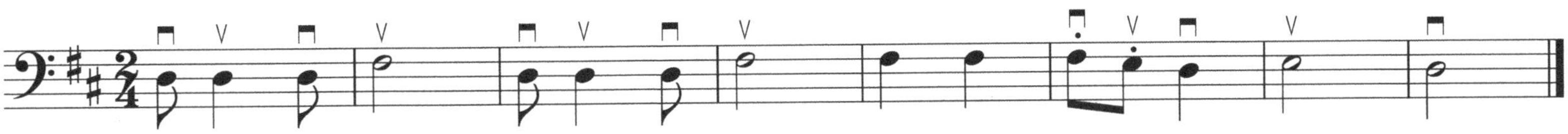

90. HOOKED ON SYNCOPATION

91. ESSENTIAL ELEMENTS QUIZ – TOM DOOLEY

American Folk Song

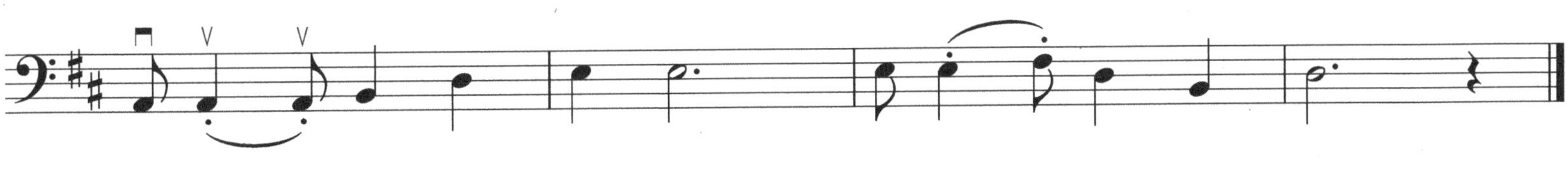

HALF POSITION ON THE A STRING

B♭

is played with 1 finger on the A string in half position (1/2).

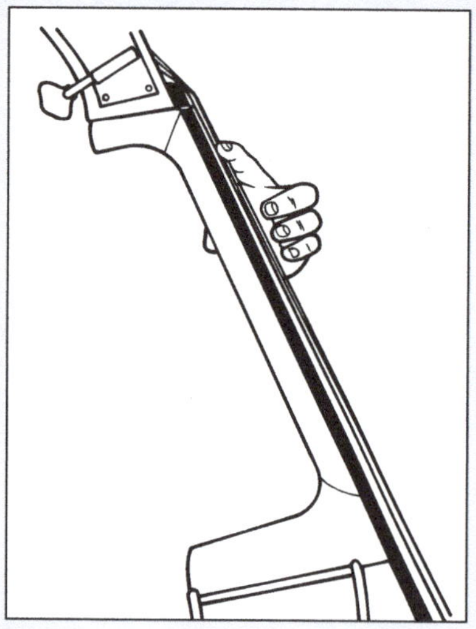

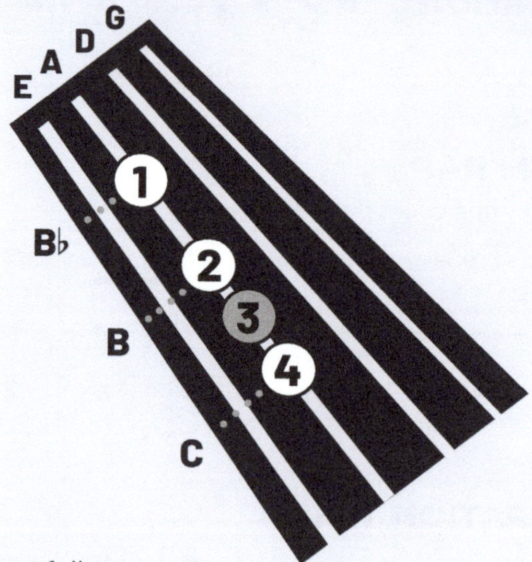

Listening Skills Play what your teacher plays. Listen carefully.

92. LET'S READ "B♭" (B-flat)

93. ROLLING ALONG

Moderato

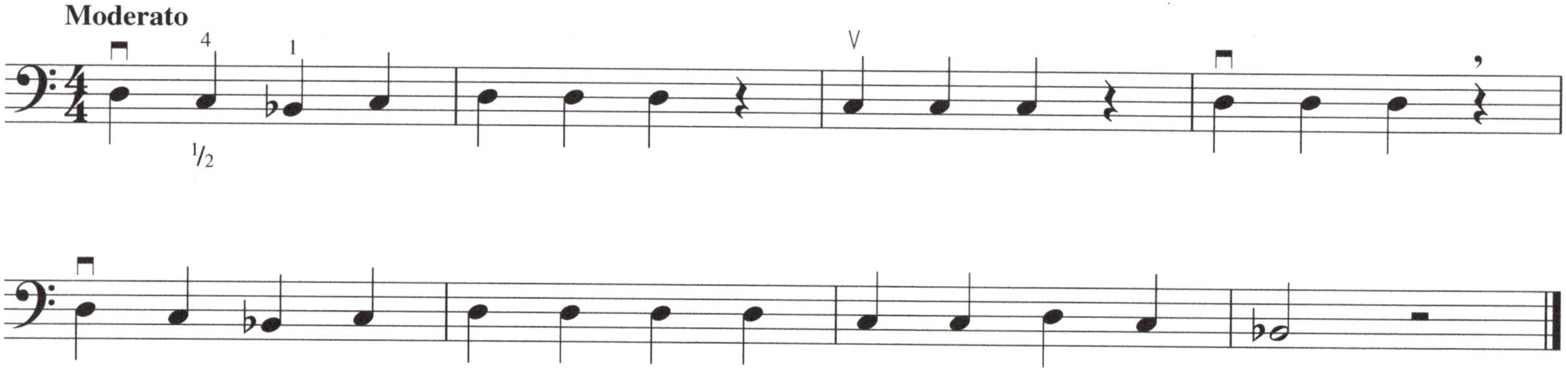

94. MATCHING OCTAVES

HALF POSITION ON THE E STRING

F

is played with 1 finger on the E string in half position (1/2).

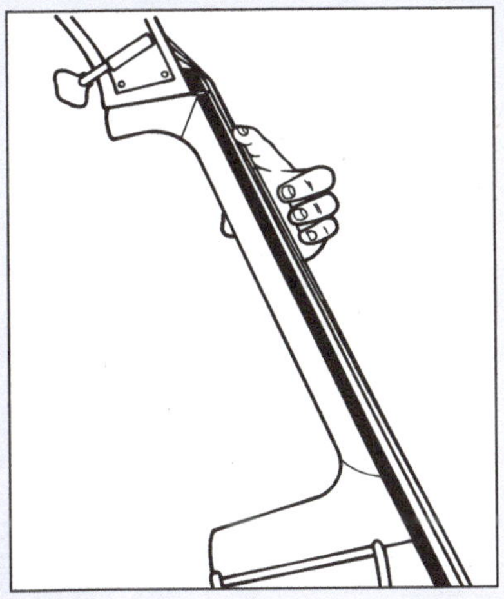

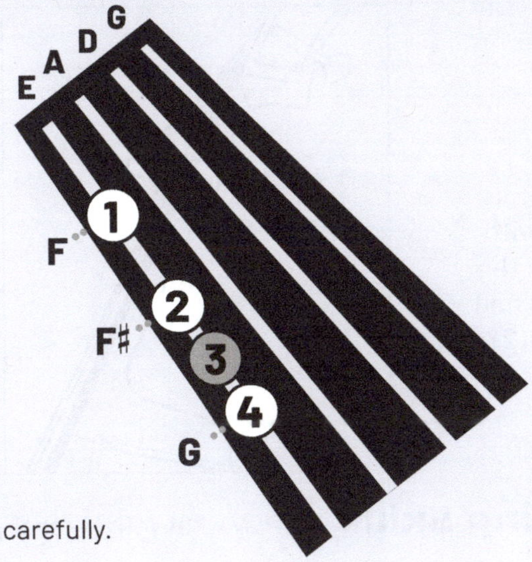

Listening Skills Play what your teacher plays. Listen carefully.

95. LET'S READ "F" (F-natural)

F

96. TECHNIQUE TRAX

THEORY

Key Signature F MAJOR

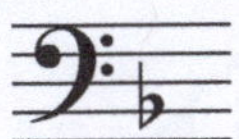

Play all B's as B♭ (B-flat).

97. F MAJOR SCALE

HISTORY

A **Concerto** is a composition in several movements for solo instrument and orchestra. Exercise 98 is the theme from the first movement of the *Concerto for Violin and Orchestra* by **Ludwig van Beethoven**, composed while author William Wordsworth was writing his poem *I Wandered Lonely as a Cloud*. A special feature of the concerto is the *cadenza*, which was improvised, or made up, by the soloist during a concert. Improvising and creating your own music is great fun. Try it if you have not already.

98. THEME FROM VIOLIN CONCERTO

Ludwig van Beethoven (1770–1827)

HALF POSITION ON THE D AND G STRINGS

E♭

is played with 1 finger on the D string in half position (1/2).

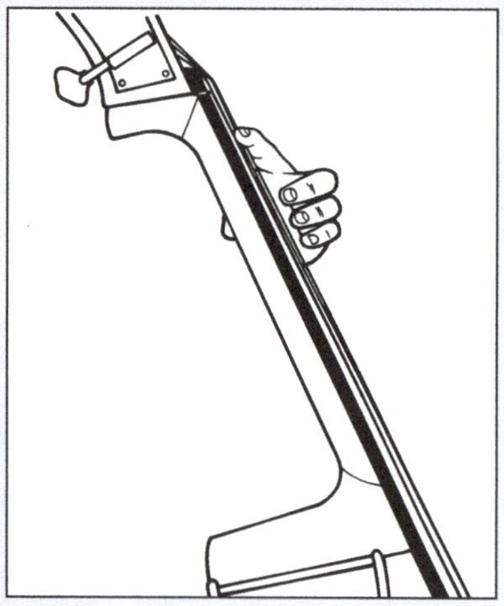

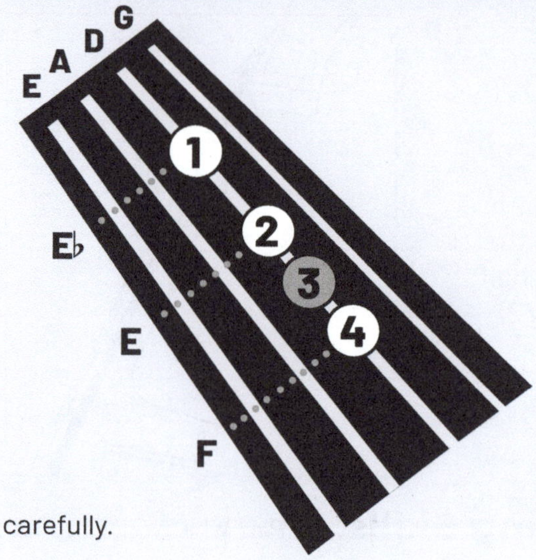

Listening Skills Play what your teacher plays. Listen carefully.

99. LET'S READ "E♭" (E-flat)

100. HOT CROSS BUNS

B♭

is played with 4 fingers on the G string in half position (1/2).

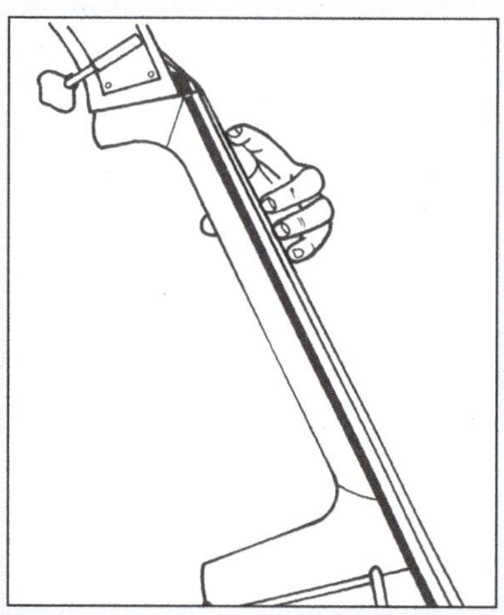

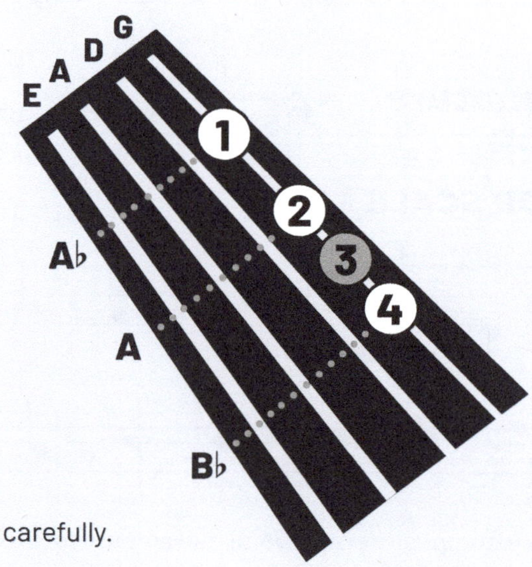

Listening Skills Play what your teacher plays. Listen carefully.

101. LET'S READ "B♭" (B-flat)

102. VIKING WAY

103. HIKING ALONG

Key Signature
B♭ MAJOR 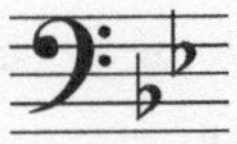 Play all B's as B♭ (B-flat) and all E's as E♭ (E-flat).

104. B♭ MAJOR SCALE

105. SLOVAKIAN FOLK SONG

106. CAVALIER COUNTRY

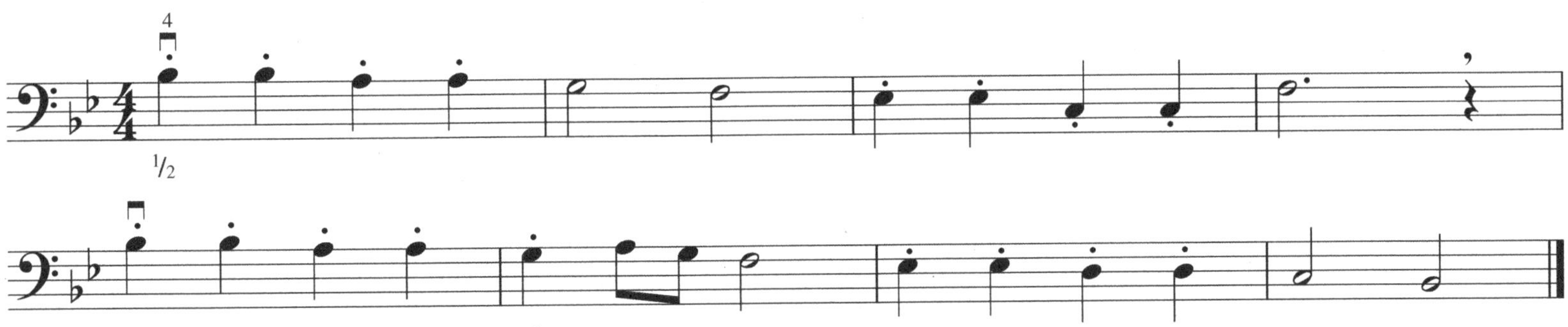

107. ESSENTIAL ELEMENTS QUIZ – AYN KAYLOKAYNU

Traditional Jewish Song

▲ *Return to original tempo*

Special Double Bass Exercise

While violins and violas are learning new notes, match the following words with the correct definitions. Write the correct letter of the definition in the blank next to the words.

1. ______ Staccato
2. ______ Allegro
3. ______ Slur
4. ______ Intonation
5. ______ Mezzo Forte
6. ______ Interval
7. ______ Crescendo
8. ______ Moderato
9. ______ Ritardando
10. ______ Allegretto
11. ______ Legato
12. ______ Fermata
13. ______ Decrescendo
14. ______ Lento
15. ______ Andante
16. ______ Tie
17. ______ Mezzo Piano
18. ______ Forte

A. Gradually increase volume
B. Hold the note (or rest) longer
C. Curved line that connects two or more different pitches
D. Play with a stopped bow stroke
E. Slower walking tempo
F. Moderately loud
G. Gradually slow the tempo
H. Play in a smooth and connected style
I. Fast tempo
J. Moderately soft
K. Curved line that connects notes of the same pitch
L. Medium tempo
M. Lively tempo, faster than Andante, but slower then Allegro
N. How well each note is played in tune
O. A very slow tempo
P. The distance between two notes
Q. Gradually decrease volume
R. Loud

108. LET'S READ "E♭" (E-flat) – Review

109. TECHNIQUE TRAX

110. LET'S READ "B♭" (B-flat) – Review

111. TECHNIQUE BUILDER

112. B♭ MAJOR SCALE

113. THE MOUNTAIN DEER CHASE

North American Folk Song

Allegretto

114. ESSENTIAL CREATIVITY – RAKES OF MALLOW

Irish Folk Song

Allegro

Music can be created and arranged by changing rhythms and notes to an existing example. Create your own arrangement of *Rakes of Mallow* by changing the rhythms and melodic phrases. Perform your arrangement for others.

Example 1: Changing rhythms

Example 2: Changing melodic phrases

THEORY

6/8 Time Signature

= **6 beats** per measure
= **Eighth** note gets one beat

♪ = 1 beat ♩ = 2 beats
♩. = 3 beats 𝅗𝅥. = 6 beats

6/8 time is usually played with a slight emphasis on the **1st** and **4th** beats of each measure.
This divides the measure into 2 groups of 3 beats each.

6/8 RHYTHMS

115. RHYTHM RAP

Shadow bow and count before playing.

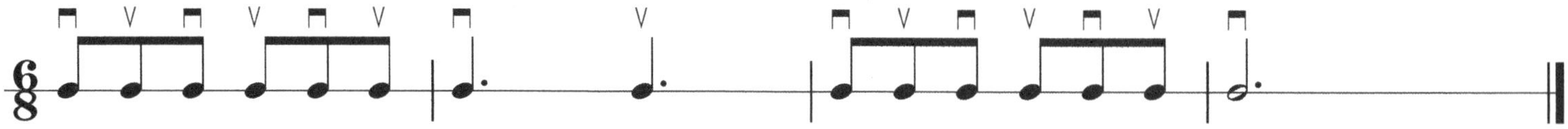

Count: **1** 2 3 **4** 5 6 **1** 2 3 **4** 5 6 **1** 2 3 **4** 5 6 **1** 2 3 **4** 5 6

116. LAZY DAY

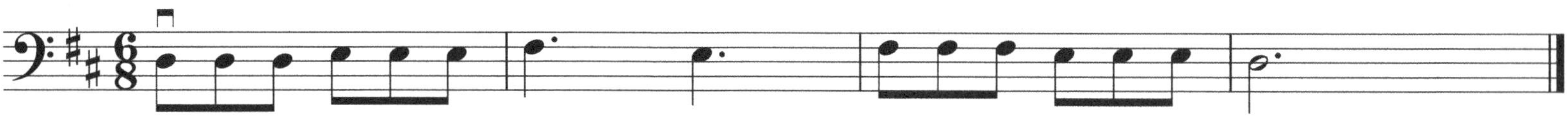

1 2 3 **4** 5 6 **1** 2 3 **4** 5 6 **1** 2 3 **4** 5 6 **1** 2 3 **4** 5 6

117. HOOKED ON 6/8

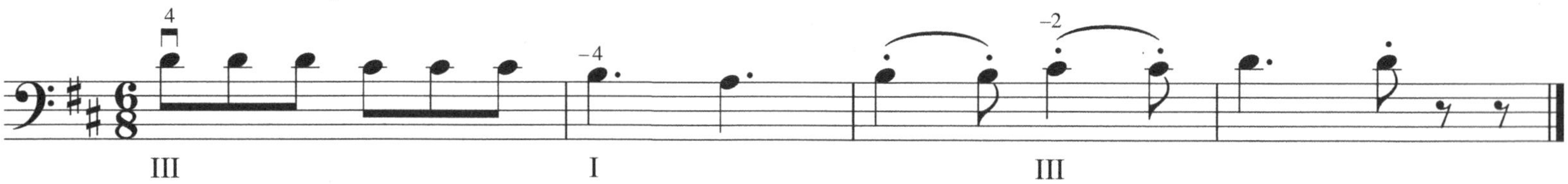

THEORY

Musical Form

A round is a **musical form** where performers play or sing the same melody, entering at different times. This is called counterpoint, a type of harmony. Try memorizing this round and performing it with a friend.

118. ROW, ROW, ROW YOUR BOAT – Round

American Folk Round

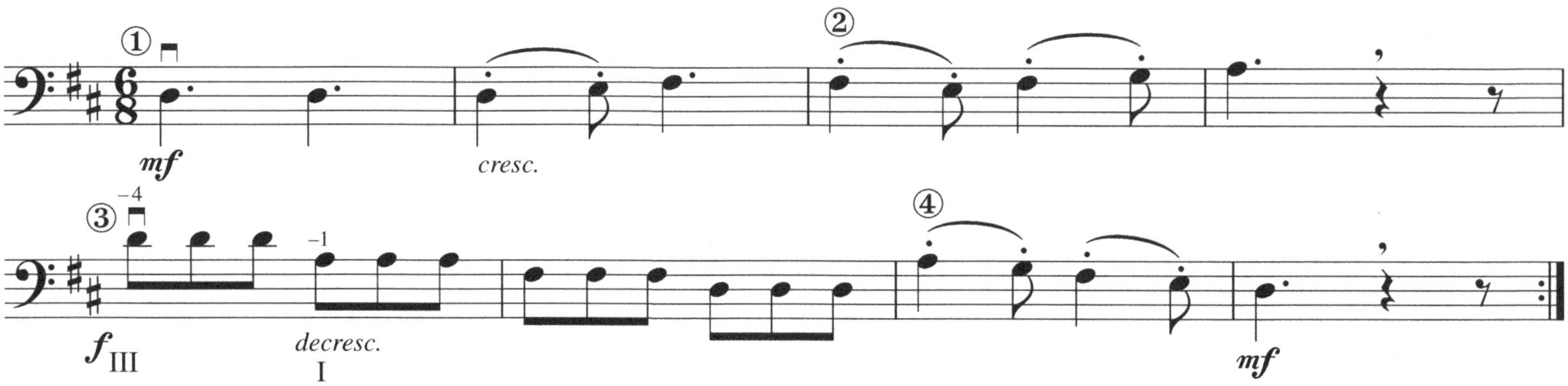

119. SLURRING IN 6/8 TIME

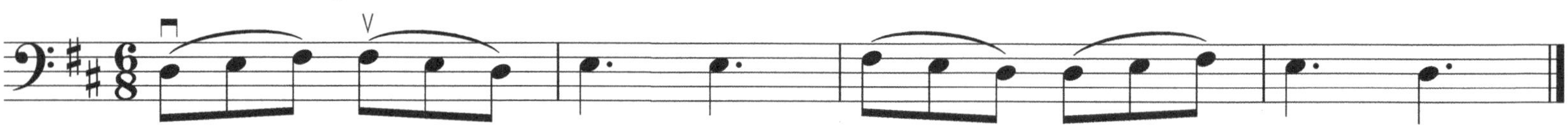

120. JOLLY GOOD FELLOW

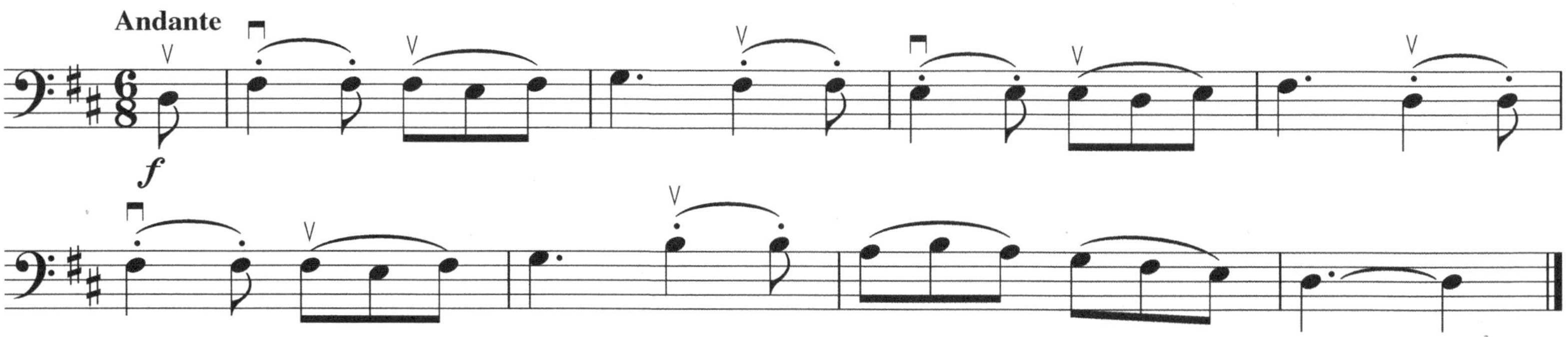

THEORY

$\frac{6}{8}$ Time Signature

When music in $\frac{6}{8}$ is played fast, it is easier to stress beats one and four, and "feel" the pulse in two large beats.

Counted in 6 = **1** 2 3 **4** 5 6

Counted in 2 = **1** & a **2** & a

6/8 RHYTHMS

121. RHYTHM RAP

Shadow bow and count before playing.

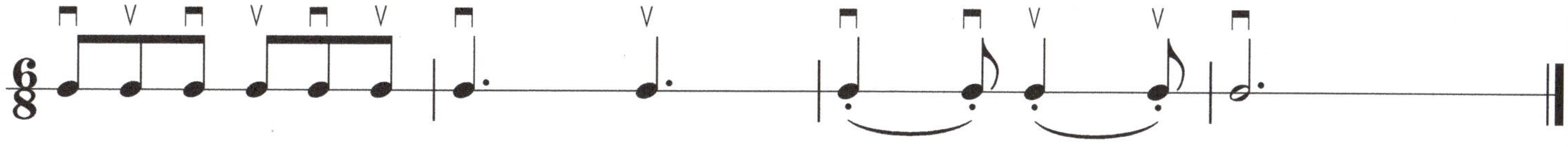

Count: **1** & a **2** & a **1** & a **2** & a **1** & a **2** & a **1** & a **2** & a

122. RISE AND FALL

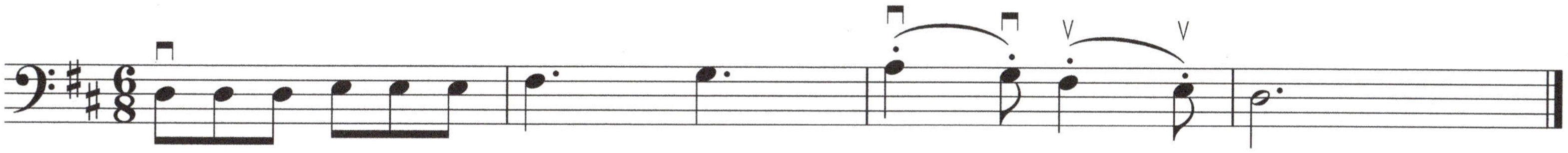

1 & a **2** & a **1** & a **2** & a **1** & a **2** & a **1** & a **2** & a

123. BEACH WALK

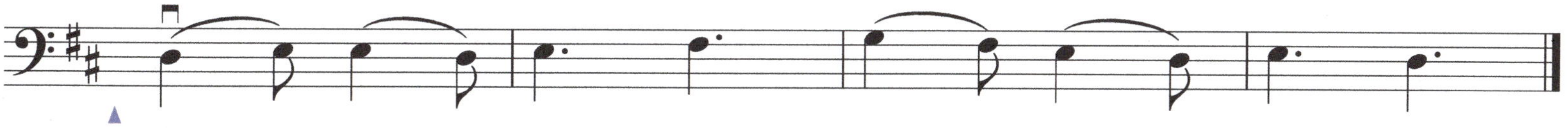

Write in the correct time signature before you begin.

HISTORY

Austrian composer **Wolfgang Amadeus Mozart** was a child prodigy who lived during the American Revolution. At five, he was composing music, and by his early teens he had mastered the violin. Mozart wrote more than 600 compositions during his short life, including oratorios, symphonies, concertos, and operas. Imagine and describe the career of a composer.

124. MAY TIME

W. A. Mozart (1756–1791)

THEORY

Minor Scale

A minor scale is a series of eight notes which follow a definite pattern of whole steps and half steps. There are three forms of the minor scale; natural minor, harmonic minor, and melodic minor. The D minor (natural) scale uses the same pitches as the F major scale.

125. D MINOR (Natural) SCALE

HISTORY

Austrian composer **Gustav Mahler** was also a successful conductor. He believed in unifying the arts and often combined music, poetry, and philosophy in his compositions. Exercise 126 *Mahler's Theme* first appears in his *Symphony No. 1*, played as a solo by the double bass. During Mahler's lifetime Vincent van Gogh created his most famous paintings, and Mark Twain wrote *Tom Sawyer*.

126. MAHLER'S THEME – Round

Gustav Mahler (1860–1911)

Andante

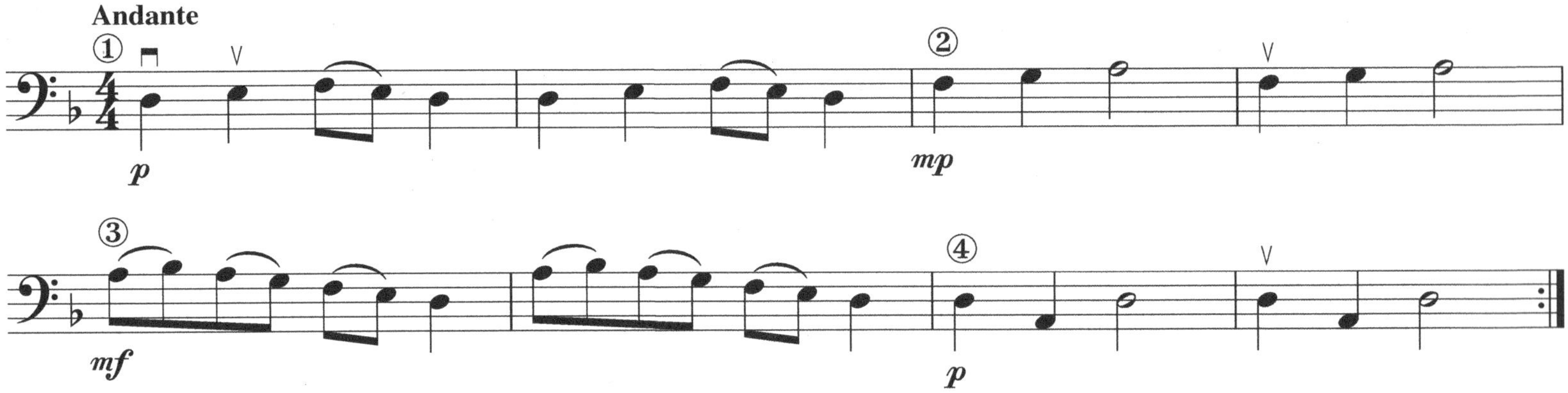

127. SHALOM CHAVERIM – Round

Hebrew Folk Song

Andante

128. THE SNAKE CHARMER

Allegretto

THEORY

Key Signature G MINOR

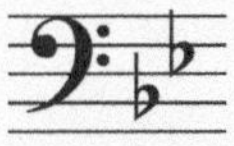

The G minor (natural) scale uses the same pitches as the B♭ major scale.

129. G MINOR (Natural) SCALE

HISTORY

With the establishment of Israel as an independent political state in 1948, *Hatikvah* became the Israeli National Anthem. This was the same year Mohandas Gandhi was assassinated in India. Israeli violinists Itzhak Perlman and Pinchas Zukerman are concert artists known throughout the world.

130. HATIKVAH

Israeli National Anthem

131. G MINOR (Natural) SCALE *(Upper Octave – violin)*

132. ESSENTIAL ELEMENTS QUIZ – THE HANUKKAH SONG

Israeli Folk Song

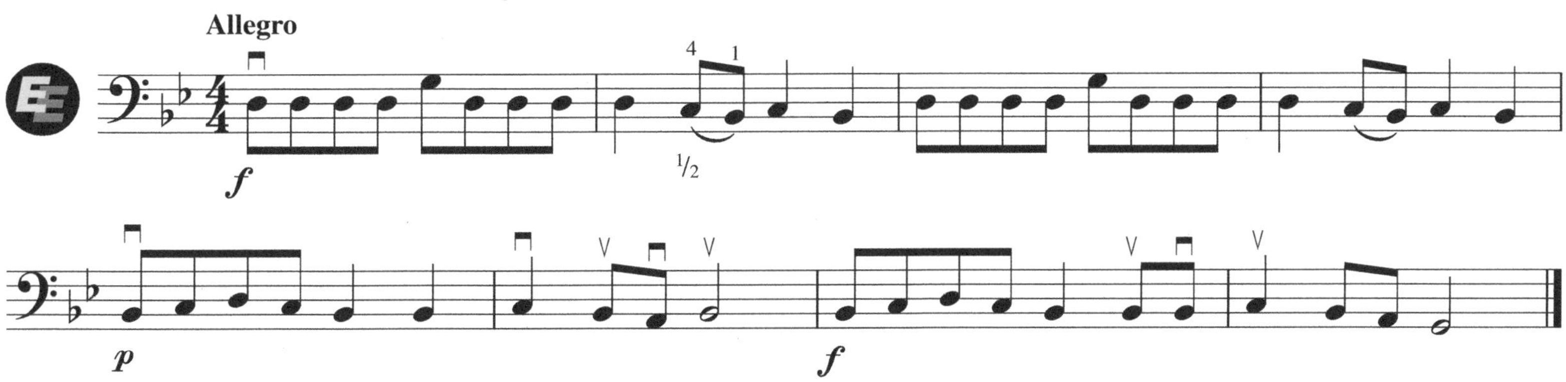

THEORY

Mixed Meter

Occasionally the meter (time signature) changes in music. Watch for meter changes and count carefully.

133. RHYTHM RAP

Shadow bow and count before playing.

Count: 1 & 2 & 3 & 4 & 1 & 2 & 3 & 4 & 1 & 2 & 3 & 1 & 2 & 3 &

134. FRENCH FOLK SONG

Moderato

THEORY

Cantabile

In a singing style.

e The Italian word for "and."

135. KUM BA YAH

African Spiritual

Andante e cantabile

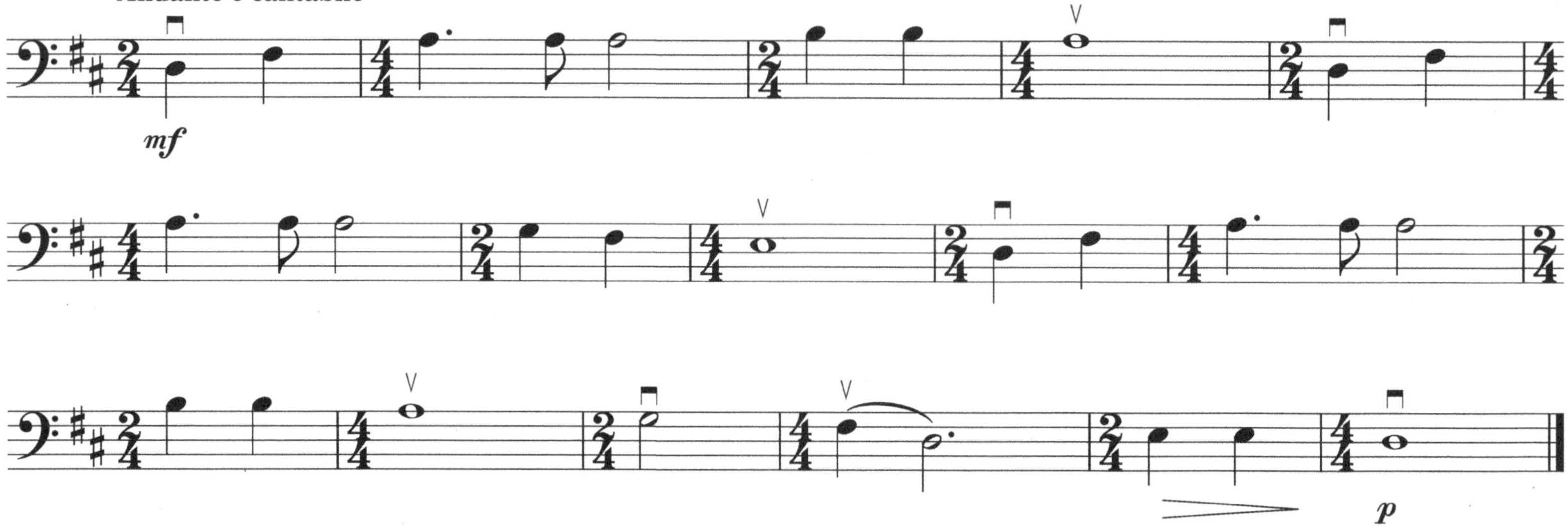

Triplets

A **triplet** is a group of **3** notes. In $\frac{2}{4}$, $\frac{3}{4}$, or $\frac{4}{4}$ time, an eighth note triplet is spread evenly across one beat.

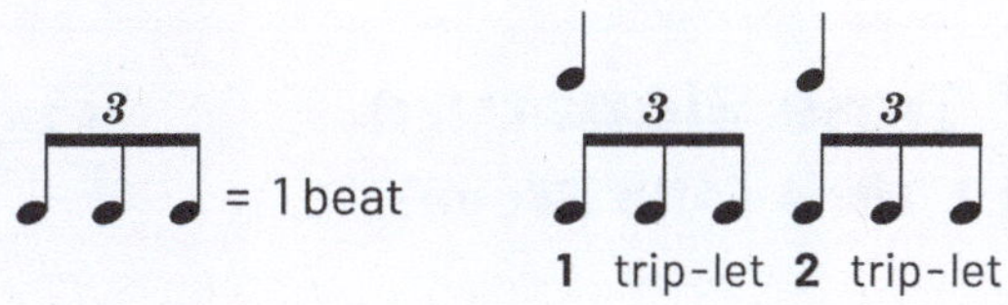

THEORY

RHYTHMS

136. RHYTHM RAP

Shadow bow and count before playing.

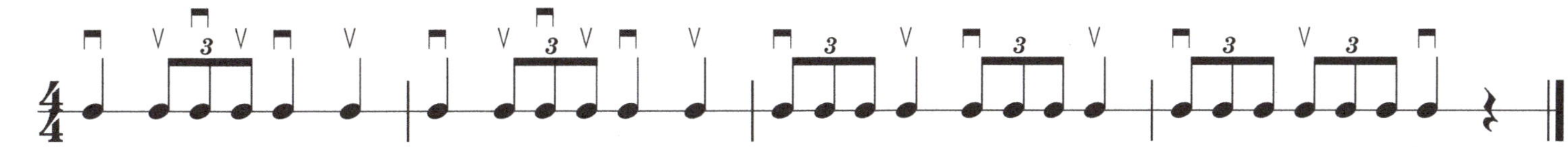

Count: **1 2 trip-let 3 4 1 2 trip-let 3 4 1 trip-let 2 3 trip-let 4 1 trip-let 2 trip-let 3 4**

137. D MAJOR SCALE WITH TRIPLETS

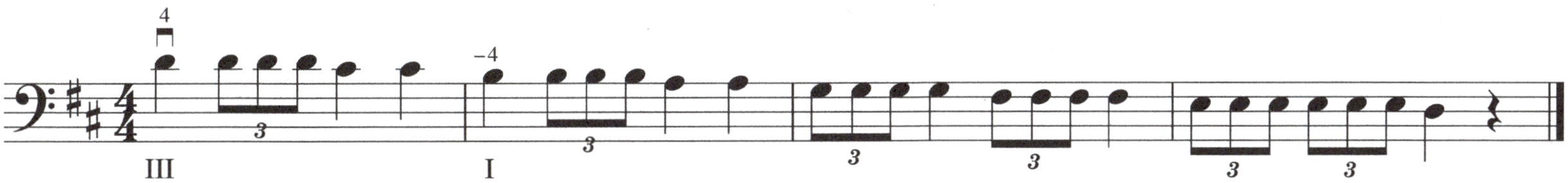

138. ON THE MOVE

139. SLURRING TRIPLETS

140. TRIPLET ETUDE

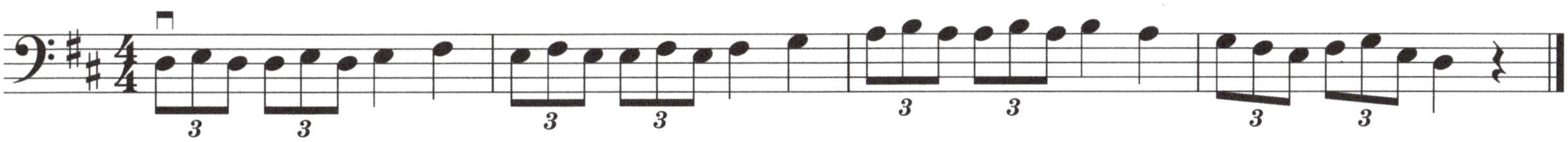

141. LITTLE RIVER

142. FIELD SONG

Southern American Folk Song

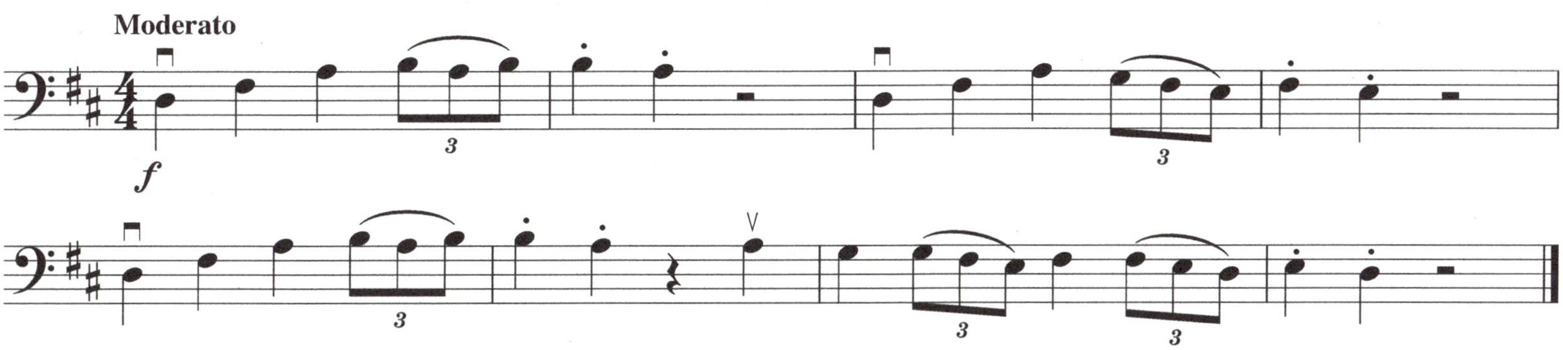

Looking for some more fun music to play?
See the inside front cover for instructions on accessing recent popular Bonus Songs.

THEORY

¢ Time Signature
Cut Time (Alla Breve)

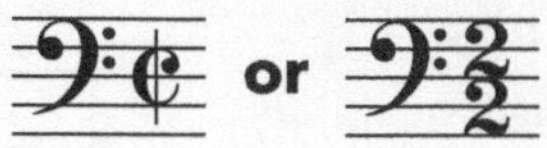

= **2 beats** per measure
= **Half** note gets one beat

whole note = 2 beats
half note = 1 beat
quarter note = ½ beat

¢ RHYTHMS

143. RHYTHM RAP
Shadow bow and count before playing.

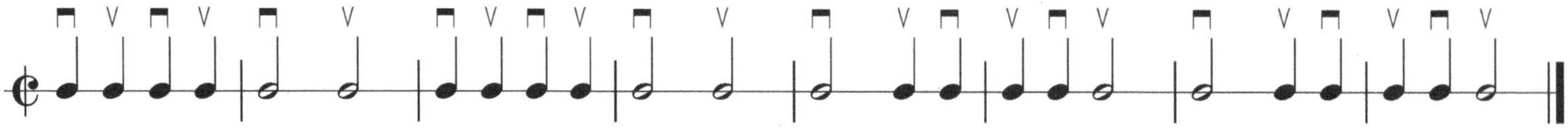

Count: 1 & 2 & 1 & 2 & 1 & 2 & 1 & 2 & 1 & 2 & 1 & 2 & 1 & 2 & 1 & 2 &

144. A CUT ABOVE

145. CUT TIME MARCH

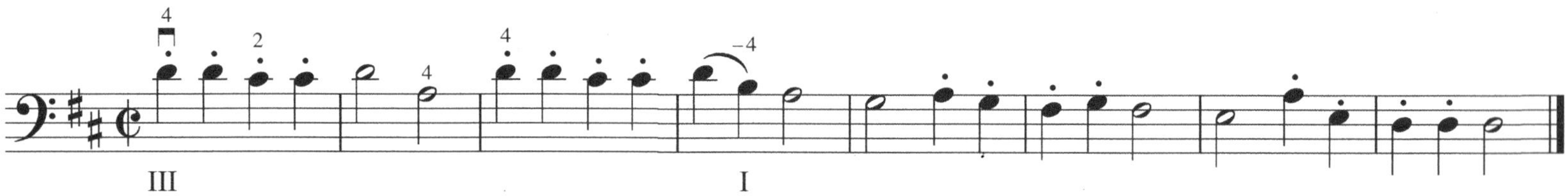

146. RHYTHM RAP
Shadow bow and count before playing.

Count: 1 & 2 & 1 & 2 & 1 & 2 & 1 & 2 & 1 & 2 & 1 & 2 & 1 & 2 & 1 & 2 &

147. SYNCOPATION MARCH

148. WHEN THE SAINTS GO MARCHIN' IN

James M. Black

Allegro

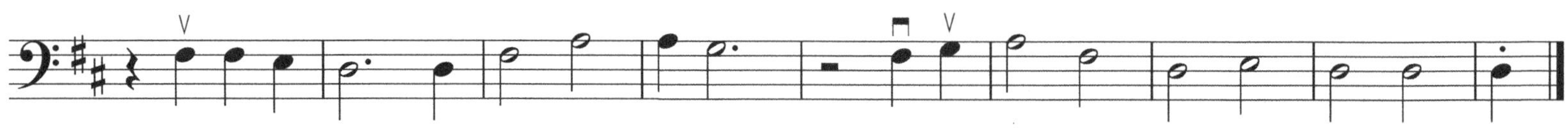

✔ Are you counting in cut time?

¢ RHYTHMS

149. RHYTHM RAP

Shadow bow and count before playing.

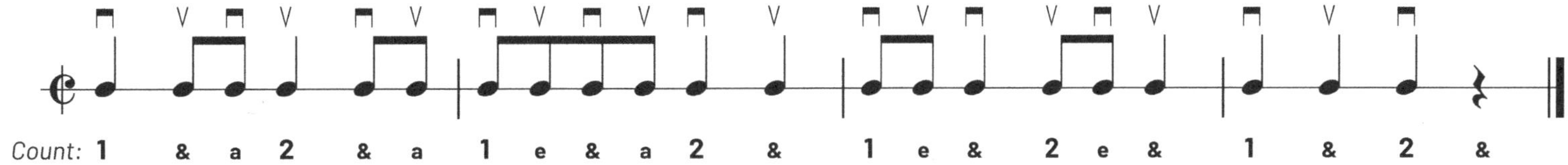

150. DOWN HOME

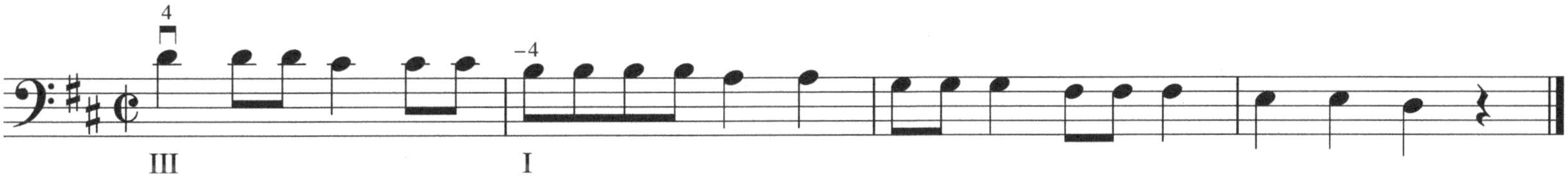

151. MOVING ALONG

152. RHYTHM RAP

Shadow bow and count before playing.

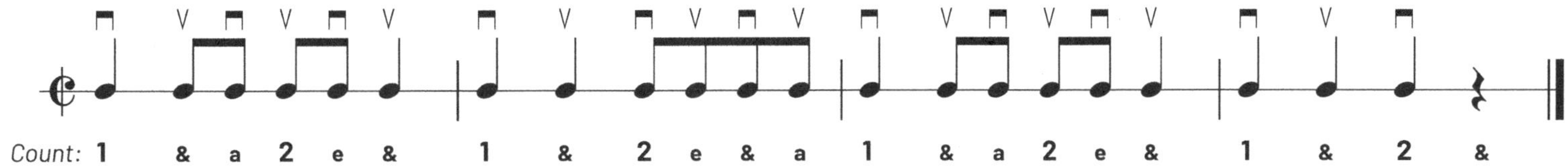

153. UP TOWN

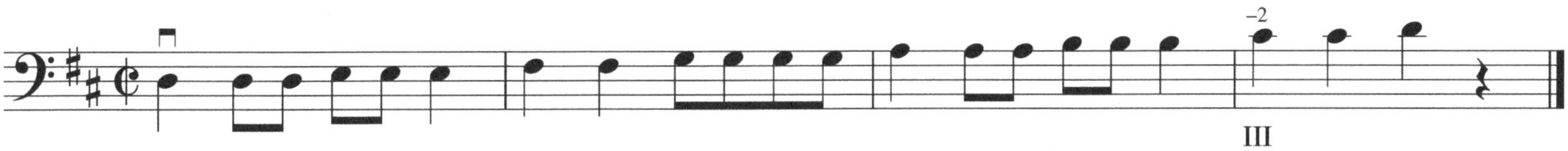

154. FLYING BOWS

HISTORY

Cantatas are pieces much like short operas that were written during the **Baroque Period** (1600–1750). They involve vocal soloists and choirs that are accompanied by small orchestras. **Johann Sebastian Bach** wrote nearly 300 of them between 1704 and 1745. While Bach was composing his cantatas, the famous philosopher Voltaire was writing his books and Thomas Jefferson, the great United States president, was born.

155. MARCH FROM PEASANT'S CANTATA

J. S. Bach (1685–1750)

PERFORMANCE SPOTLIGHT

Performing music for others is fun and rewarding. Either small or large ensembles can perform the following arrangements. Always observe proper concert etiquette by being well prepared, dressing appropriately, being on time, and remembering all equipment. Show respect when others are playing by listening attentively and applauding at the appropriate time.

156. SAGEBRUSH OVERTURE – Orchestra Arrangement **A** = Melody part. **B** = Orchestra part.

Arr. John Higgins

✓ What were the strong points of your performance?

157. POMP AND CIRCUMSTANCE – Orchestra Arrangement

Edward Elgar (1857–1933)
Arr. John Higgins

A = Melody part. **B** = Orchestra part.

158. AMERICA THE BEAUTIFUL – Orchestra Arrangement

Samuel Augustus Ward (1847–1903)
Arr. John Higgins

A = Melody part. **B** = Orchestra part.

159. LA BAMBA – Duet

Mexican Folk Song
Arr. Michael Allen

PERFORMANCE SPOTLIGHT

HISTORY

Gustav Holst was a famous British orchestra composer who frequently set words to music, including poems by the American poet, Walt Whitman. Holst's *St. Paul's Suite* for string orchestra was written for the St. Paul's Girls School Orchestra and published in 1913. His best known work is *The Planets*, first performed in 1918, the same year as the end of World War I.

160. THE BLEAK MIDWINTER – Orchestra Arrangement

A = Melody part. **B** = Orchestra part.

Gustav Holst (1874–1934)
Arr. John Higgins

161. SWALLOWTAIL JIG – Orchestra Arrangement

Irish Jig
Arr. John Higgins

A = Melody part. **B** = Orchestra part.

Sight-reading

Sight-reading means playing a musical piece for the first time. The key to sight-reading success is to know what to look for *before* you play. Use the word **S-T-A-R-S** to remind yourself what to look for, and eventually your orchestra will become sight-reading STARS!

- **S** – **Sharps or flats** in the key signature
- **T** – **Time signature** and **tempo markings**
- **A** – **Accidentals** not found in the key signature
- **R** – **Rhythms**, silently counting the more difficult notes and rests
- **S** – **Signs**, including dynamics, articulations, repeats and endings

162. SIGHT-READING CHALLENGE #1

163. SIGHT-READING CHALLENGE #2

164. SIGHT-READING CHALLENGE #3

165. SIGHT-READING CHALLENGE #4

PREPARING FOR HIGHER POSITIONS

Natural Harmonic

Natural harmonics are tones created by a vibrating string divided into equal sections. To play an octave higher than an open string, lightly touch the string exactly half way between the bridge and the nut. In the following examples, harmonics are indicated by a "o" above a note, plus a fingering number. $\overset{3}{\circ}$ indicates a harmonic played with the third finger.

166.

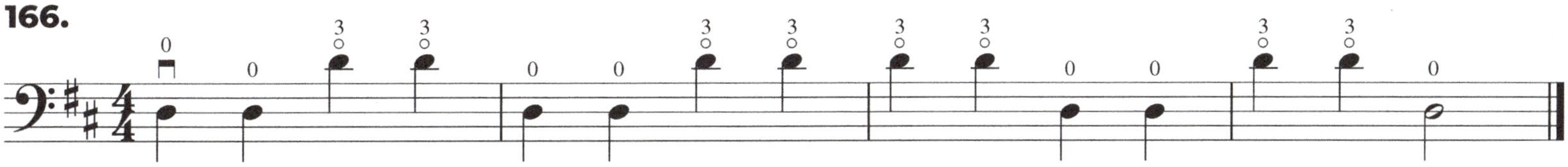

167.

168.

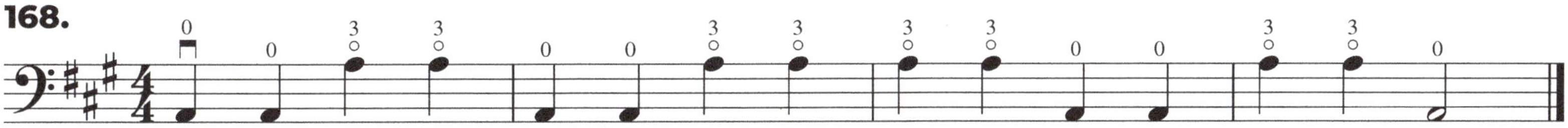

169.

Shifting

Sliding your left hand smoothly and lightly to a new location on the fingerboard, indicated by a dash (–). Be sure your thumb moves with your hand.

170.

171.

172.

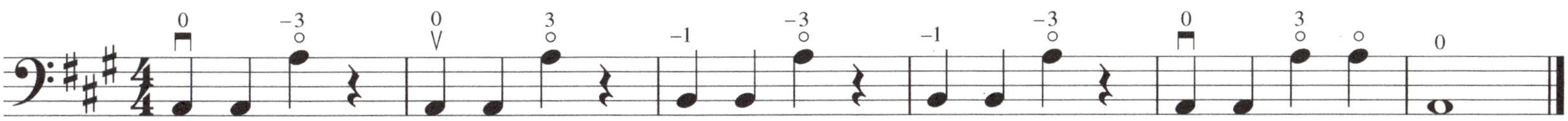

173.

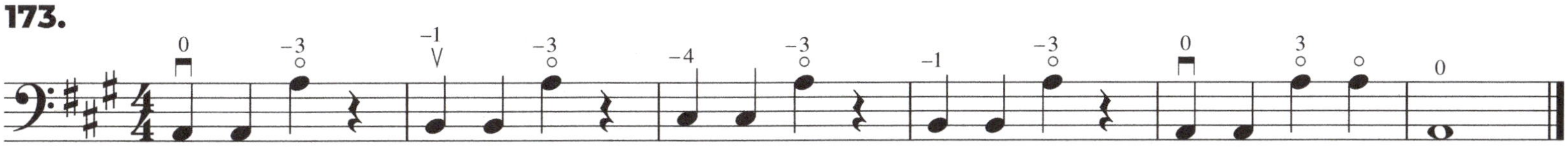

FINGER PATTERNS (violin and viola)

While the violins and violas are practicing various finger patterns, you will be playing some new notes in new positions. All new positions are indicated with a ★ and shifts with a –. Remember to slide your hand smoothly and lightly to the new location. Always keep your thumb behind your second finger.

FINGER PATTERNS (By Pattern)

174. 3–4 PATTERN *(violin, viola)*

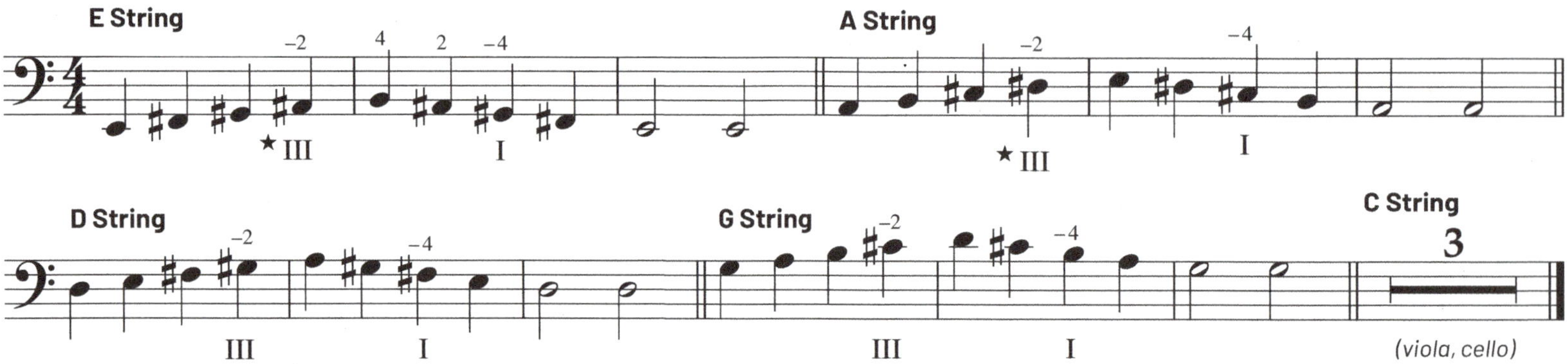

175. 2–3 PATTERN *(violin, viola)*

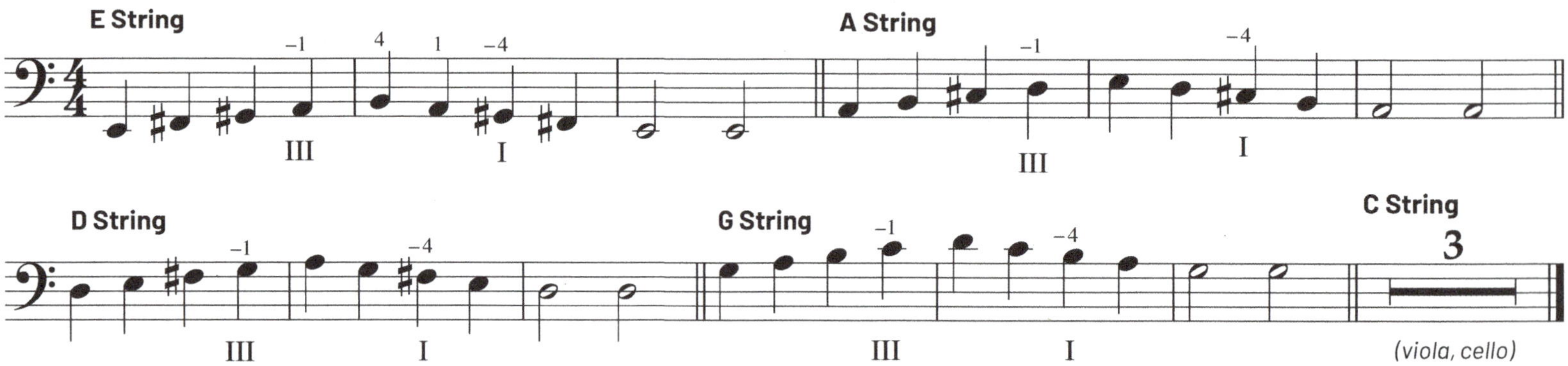

176. 1–2 PATTERN *(violin, viola)*

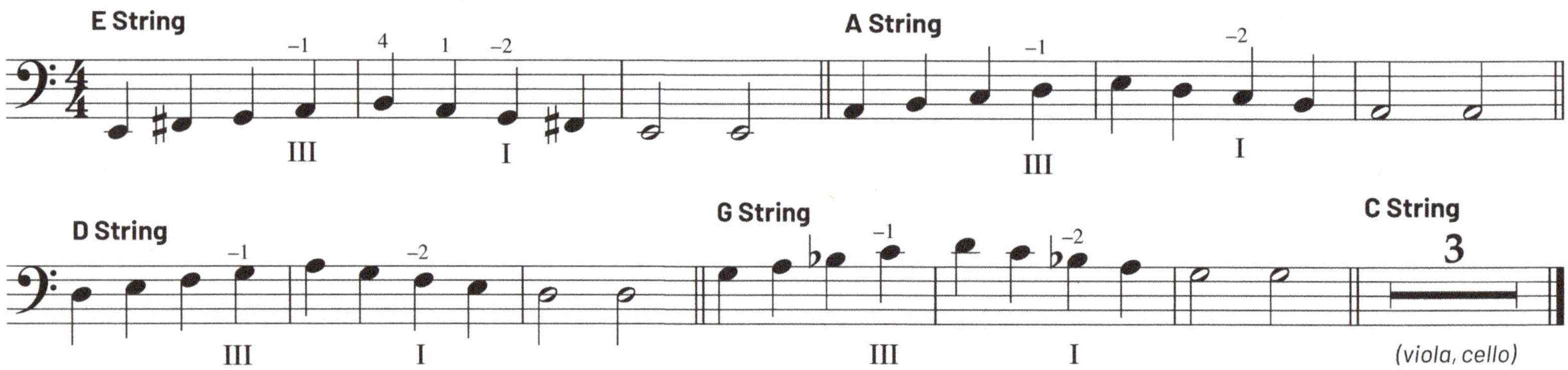

177. OPEN PATTERN *(violin, viola)*

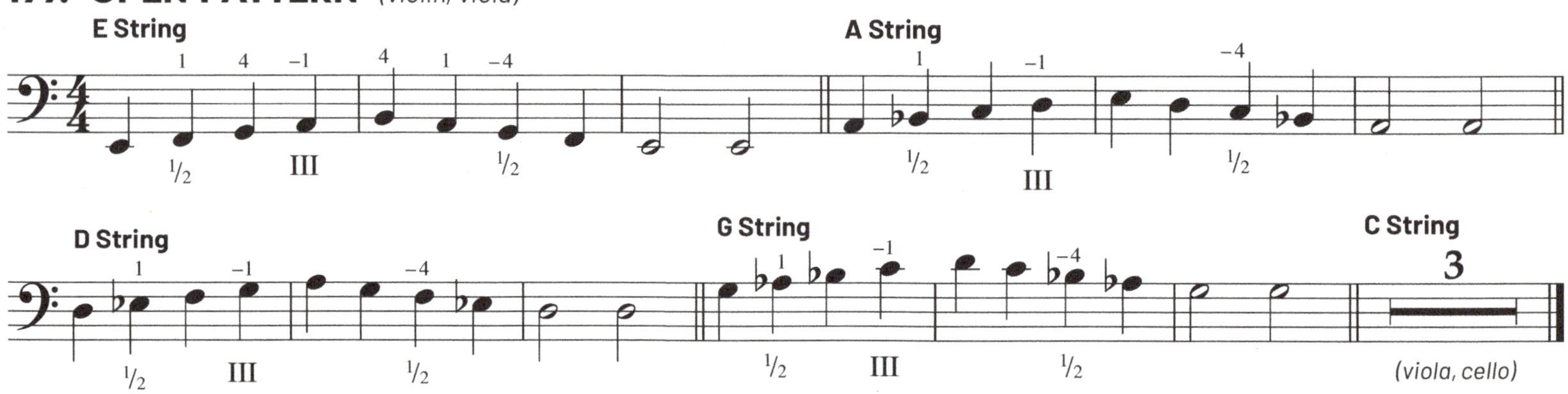

FINGER PATTERNS (By String)

178. E STRING

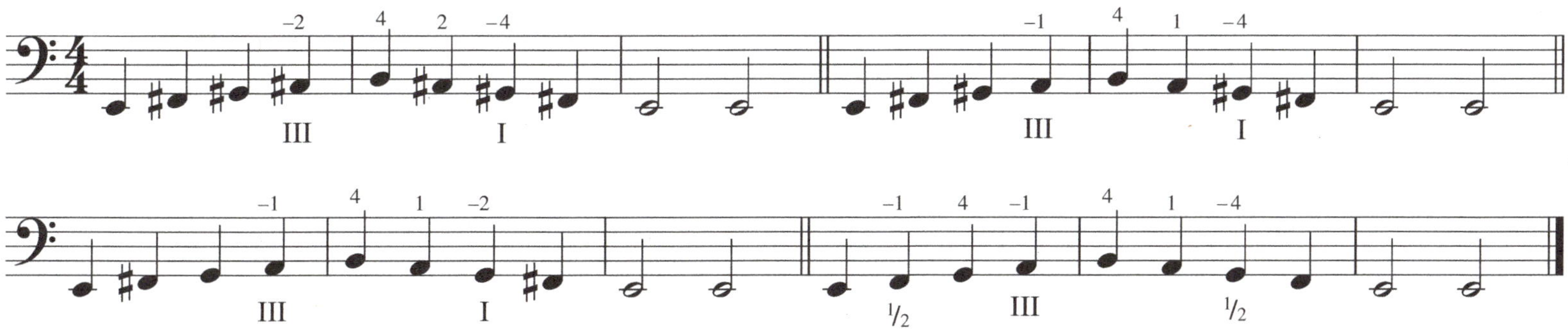

179. A STRING

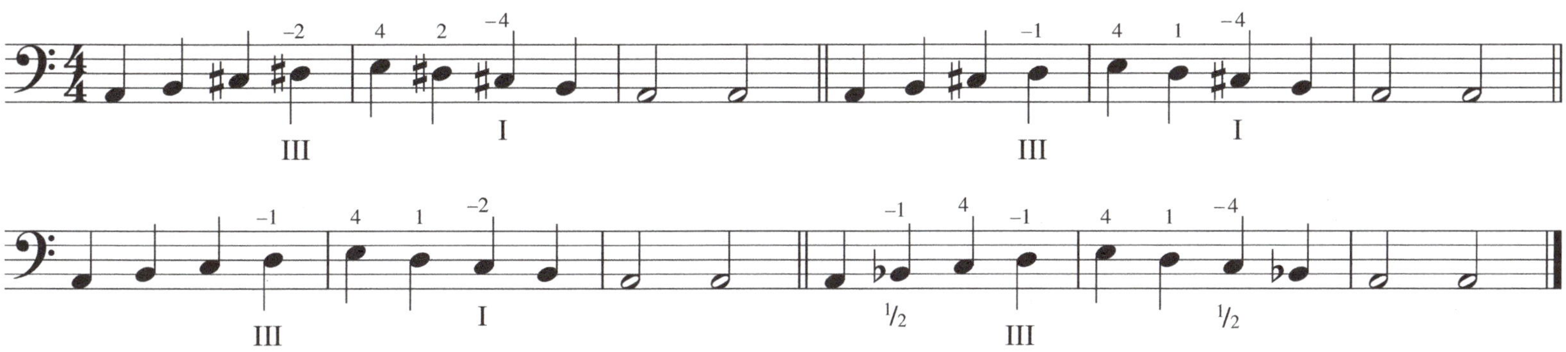

180. D STRING

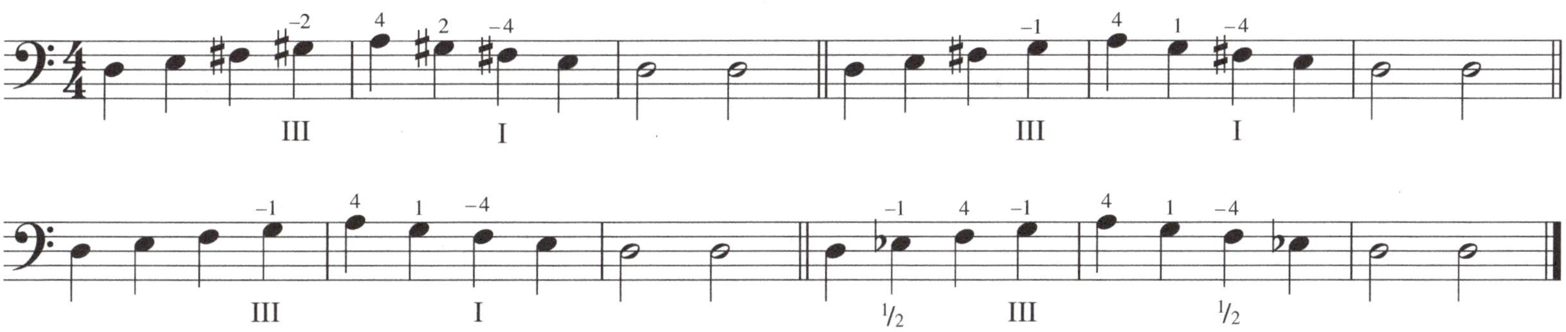

181. G STRING

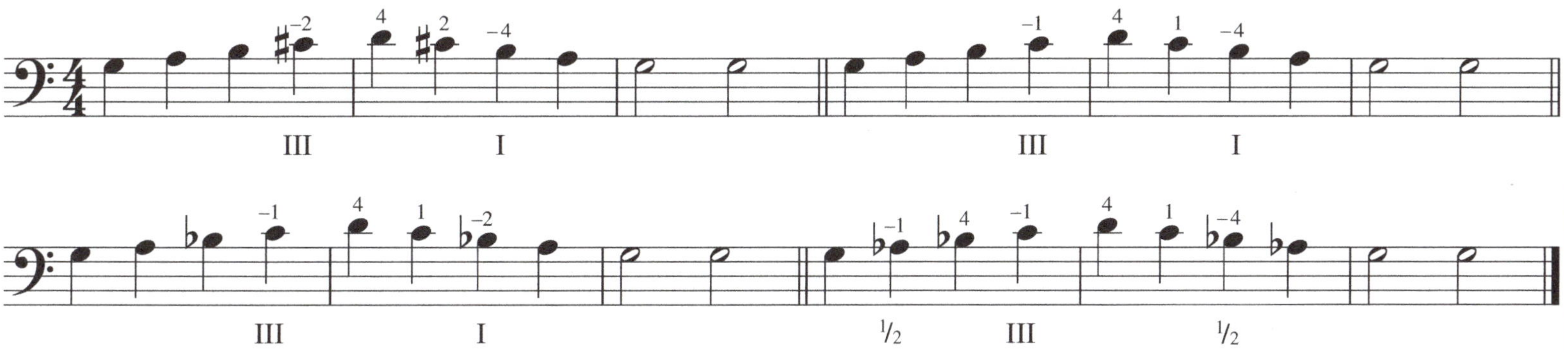

182. C STRING *(viola, cello)*

FINGER PATTERNS (By Key)

183. C MAJOR

184. G MAJOR

185. D MAJOR

186. A MAJOR

187. F MAJOR

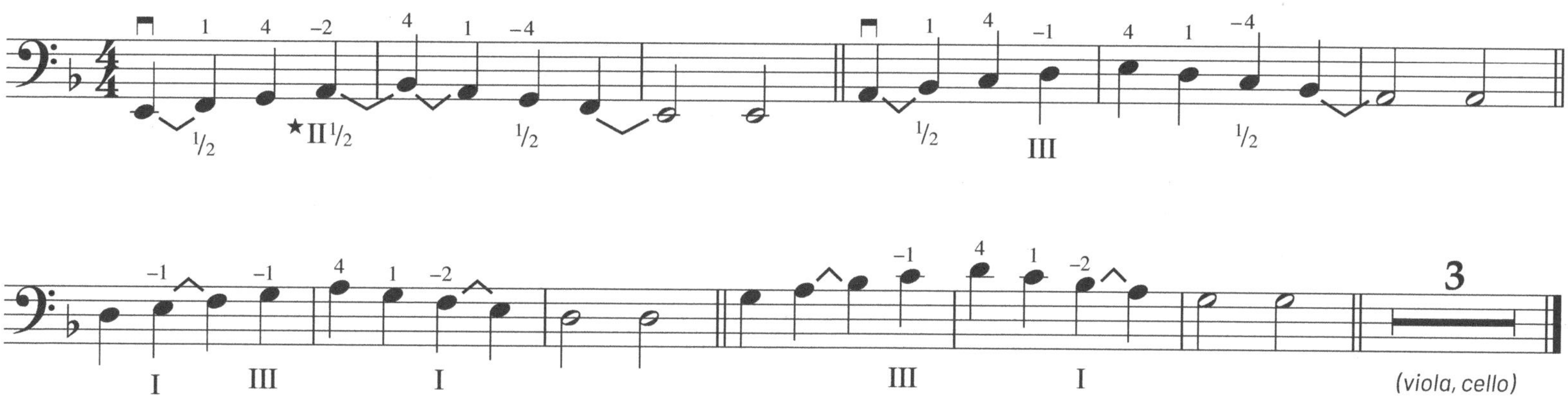

188. B♭ MAJOR

SCALES AND ARPEGGIOS

✔ Identify two important elements of performing scales and arpeggios accurately.
As you play each line, check to make sure you are able to do these things.

189. C MAJOR

190. C MAJOR *(Lower Octave - viola and cello)*

191. G MAJOR

192. G MAJOR *(Upper Octave - violin)*

193. D MAJOR

194. D MAJOR *(Lower Octave - viola and cello)*

195. A MAJOR

196. A MAJOR *(Upper Octave - violin)*

197. F MAJOR

198. B♭ MAJOR

199. B♭ MAJOR *(Upper Octave - violin)*

200. D MINOR (Natural)

201. D MINOR (Natural) *(Lower Octave – viola and cello)*

202. G MINOR (Natural)

203. G MINOR (Natural) *(Upper Octave - violin)*

CREATING MUSIC

THEORY

Improvisation

Improvisation is the art of freely creating your own music as you play.

204. *Using the following notes, improvise your own melody (Line A) to go with the accompaniment (Line B).*

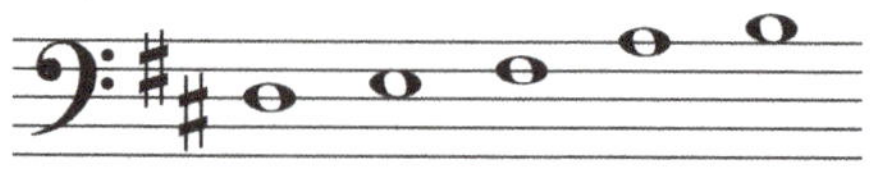

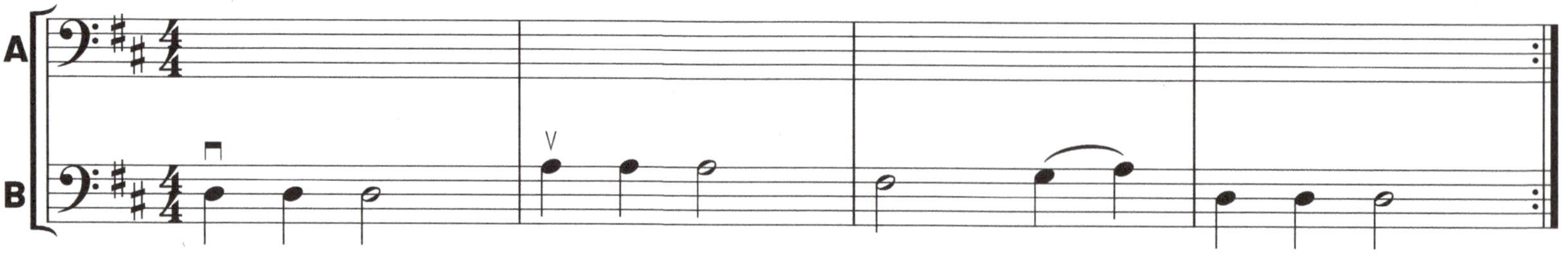

THEORY

Composition

Composition is the art of writing original music. A composer often begins by creating a melody made up of individual **phrases**, like short musical "sentences." Some melodies have phrases that seem to answer or respond to "question" phrases, as in Beethoven's *Ode To Joy*. Play this melody and listen to how phrase 2 answers phrase 1.

205. ODE TO JOY

Ludwig van Beethoven (1770–1827)

1. Question

2. Answer

206. PHRASE BUILDERS

Write 2 different phrases using the following rhythms.

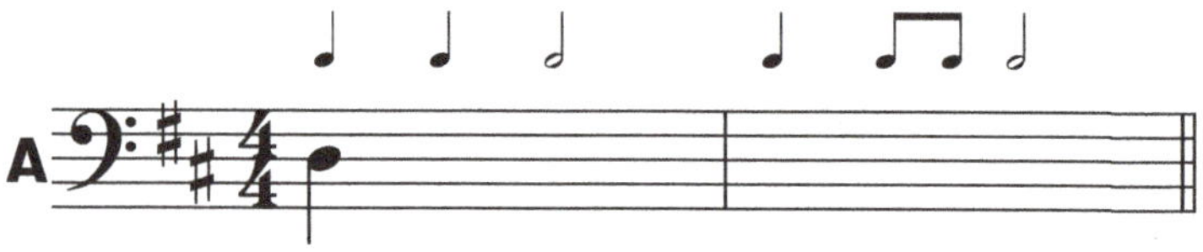

207. Q. AND A.

Write your own "answer" to the following melodies.

1. Question *2. Answer*

1. Question *2. Answer*

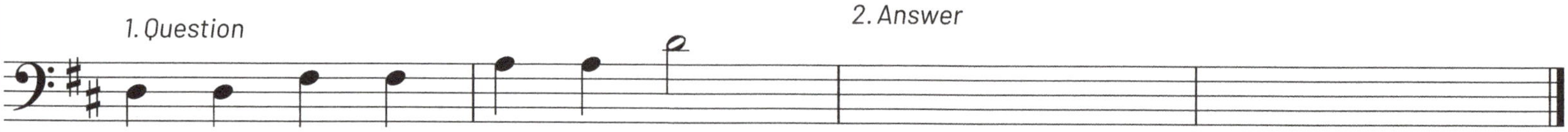

208. YOU NAME IT: ______________________

Now write your own music.

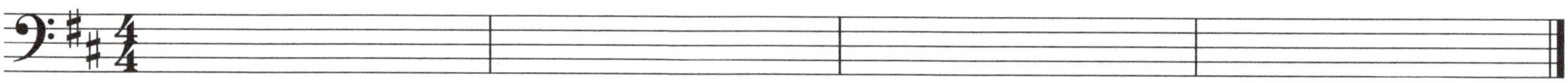

IMPROVISATION/COMPOSITION

Double Stops

A **double stop** is playing two strings at once.

209. TWO AT A TIME

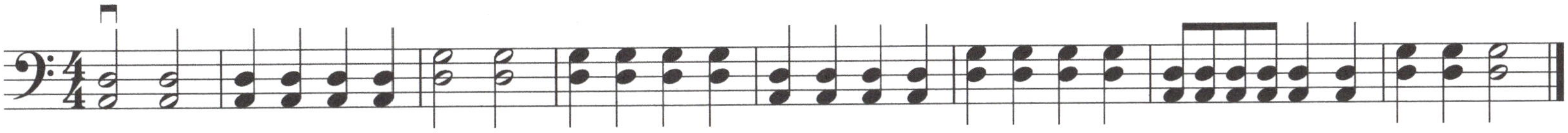

210. ADDING FINGERS

DOUBLE BASS FINGERING CHART

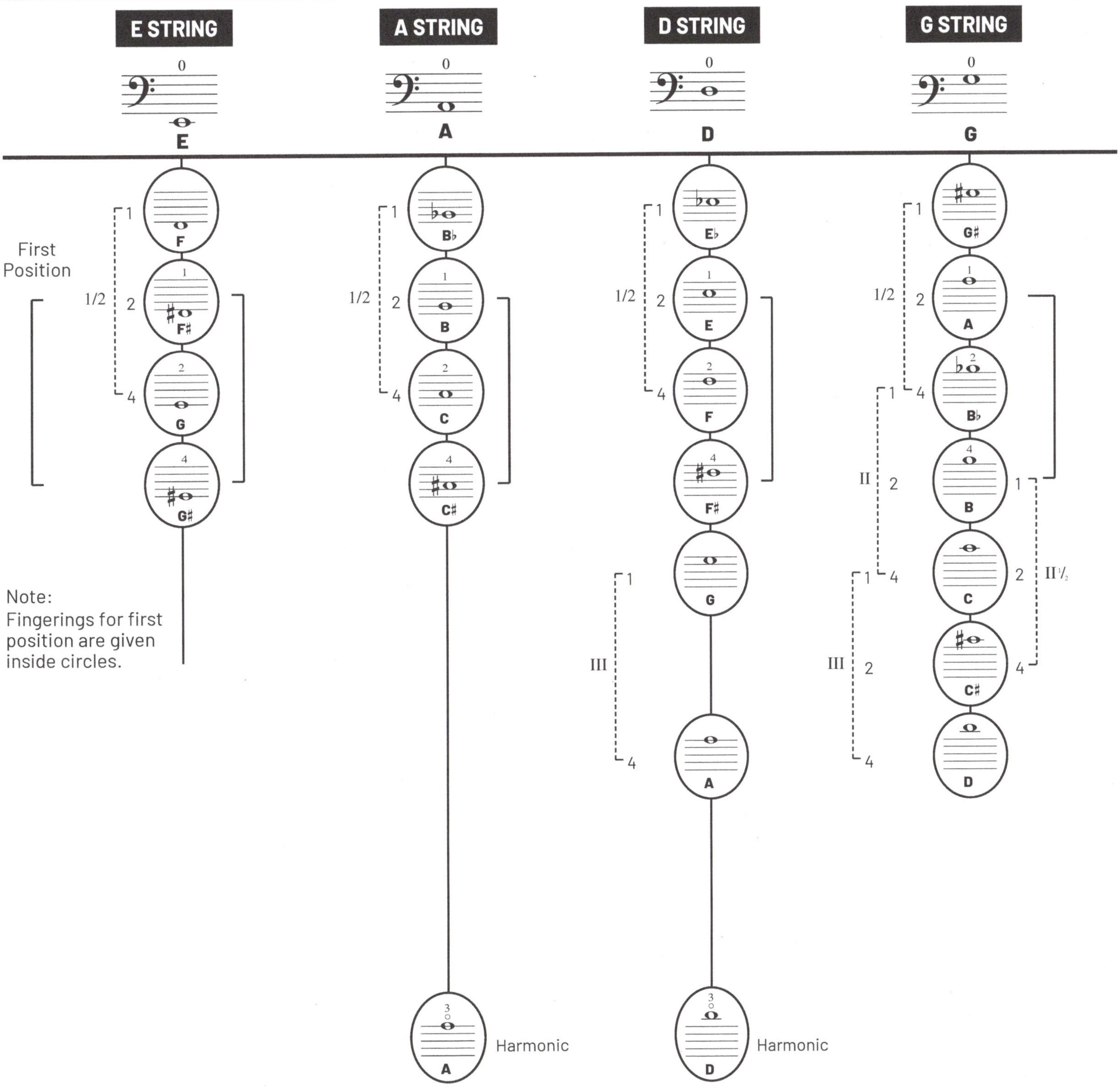

Reference Index